Country Suppers

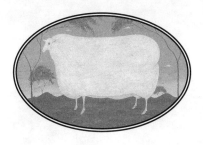

Best Wishes,

Ruth Cousineau

Country Suppers

Simple, Hearty Fare for Family & Friends

Ruth Cousineau

Illustrations by
Warren Kimble

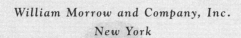

William Morrow and Company, Inc.
New York

It is the policy of William Morrow and Company, Inc., and its imprints and
affiliates, recognizing the importance of preserving what has been written, to
print the books we publish on acid-free paper, and we exert our best efforts
to that end.

Library of Congress Cataloging-in-Publication Data

Cousineau, Ruth.
    Country suppers : simple, hearty fare for family and friends / by Ruth
Cousineau ; illustrations by Warren Kimble.—1st ed.
        p.   cm.
    Includes bibliographical references and index.
    ISBN 0-688-15223-6
    1. Suppers.   I. Title.
TX738.C68   1997
641.5'3—DC21   97-7232
                                                                 CIP

Printed in the United States of America

First Edition

1   2   3   4   5   6   7   8   9   10

BOOK DESIGN BY RICHARD ORIOLO

This book is dedicated to Len,

who keeps me company.

Acknowledgments

I WOULD LIKE TO thank the many people who have helped with recipes, advice, and friendship. First of all my editor, Pam Hoenig, and her assistant, Naomi Glikman, for sure-headed guidance; Meg Ruley, my agent, who won't take no for an answer; and Warren and Lorraine Kimble, for their support and joy and wonderful art work. Thanks to Len Cousineau, Pamela Inkley, and especially Angela Combes for proofreading and cheerful, helpful commentary. Many thanks to Mary Jirik, Jeannette Kling, Trish Norton, Jessica Reisman, Tom Austin, Rob McKain, Matt Beebe, Jan Edwards, Stark Biddle, Sharon Nimtz, Jake Sherman, Michael Wells, Andy Snyder, Helen Snyder, and Chris Anderson for sharing their recipes and good chats. *Mille mercies* to Jay Weiss *pour tous les bons mots.* Thanks to Sandy Gluck and Ralph Stieber around whose supper table I have spent many wonderful moments of friendship. Years of thanks to my mother, Muriel Reisman, and my mother-in-law, Mary Cousineau, for sharing both their love and their knowledge of cooking. And my thanks to all those friendly folks who sat at tables with us at community suppers all over Vermont, sharing memories, recipes, and good food.

Contents

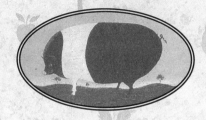

Introduction

IT WAS A BLUSTERY February afternoon and we had a bad case of cabin fever. "We'll go somewhere for supper. Have a look in the paper for the nearest one," I said to my husband. There was a chicken-and-biscuit supper two towns down the road from us in Middletown Springs at five o'clock. In the basement of St. Ann's Church we found tables set with silverware and bowls of pickles. Soon friendly faces were ladling out a delicious supper. We joined some folks at one table and they knew our next-door neighbors. The food was good and the conversation better!

Supper should be a rather simple but hearty meal, the foods comforting and tasting like home. In Vermont we invite people in for supper or we go out—out to church suppers, potluck suppers, tasting suppers, Town Meeting suppers, and covered-dish suppers. A look in any local paper at any time of the year finds notices for just plain suppers, roast beef suppers, roast pork suppers, game suppers, and ham suppers. Then there are chicken barbecues, fish fries, pie auctions, endless bake sales, and my favorite, the turkey social.

Many of these suppers have their roots in seasonal harvest celebrations. We have apples and pumpkins galore in autumn, and in the muddy days of March and April, we boil sap to make maple syrup. Nowadays, these suppers are often held as fund-raisers as well as being convivial outings for communities and an enjoyable way to spread around the excess. Strawberry socials in the beginning of July and game suppers in late fall are just two examples.

Searching out these suppers gives us an opportunity to explore Vermont's villages and hamlets. One popular ham supper is held in a beautifully spare Congregational church that doubles as the town hall, overlooking mountain views to the east. Community suppers also allow visitors to participate in genuine Vermont life often not far off the tourists' well-beaten path.

Vermont has long seasons of dark nights that need enlivening by the company of friends. Having people in for supper is one of the best ways I know of to cure the winter blahs. One feels comforted by the warming hearty foods served at home. I find much pleasure serving a warm blueberry cobbler, made from blueberries grown on the slope behind our house, and remembering sunny summer days.

Cooking is not only a creative process, but one that connects us to our basic need for food. When it is done as a chore or in the spirit of disinterest, no one wants to do it. But I see the process as a gift, one that connects me to the effort of the farmer, the butcher, the vintner, and all those who cultivate the land and produce by hard labor the food we enjoy.

I know everyone is busy these days, since people are always asking me for quick recipes. I think a great deal about this need for speed, and some recipes in this book are indeed fast, while others will take some time—time that you can use to enjoy the process, sip a little wine, and smell those good aromas that bring people into the kitchen, sniffing and asking, "What's cooking?"

Supper means sharing with family, friends, and strangers who become friends. It is difficult to sit down at a long table of strangers and not start talking. I have chosen dishes that represent many of those served at Vermont suppers as well as some favorites from the tables of family and friends to share with you. This cookbook is written to remember and preserve some skills from the past, to pass on a connection from great-grandparents to their granddaughters and sons, and to celebrate the sense of community that exists in my home state. So, the next time you are asked to bring a dish to a potluck supper or invite your friends in for supper, you will be able to serve a bit of Vermont!

—RUTH COUSINEAU

What's in the Cupboard?

H ERE IS A LIST of ingredients that are in my cupboard, and might not be in yours. These are my basic tools, and understanding how to use them will make your cooking easier and hopefully more pleasurable.

Arrowroot, cornstarch, and tapioca: These are starches that are used as thickening agents for gravies, sauces, puddings, and pies. Each has its own characteristics and you should experiment to see which ones you like in particular dishes. I like to mix cornstarch and tapioca when thickening pies, because I find this produces the consistency I want. When I need a very delicate thickener, I choose arrowroot, available in the spice section of the supermarket.

Stock, chicken, beef, and lamb: Homemade tastes better than canned broth. Save bones in the freezer, and when you have accumulated 3 to 4 pounds, put them in a stockpot with cold water to cover, add a carrot, an onion, and a celery stalk, and bring to a boil. Skim off any foam that rises, reduce the heat, and simmer for several hours. Strain the stock through a paper towel–lined sieve, cool, and freeze in pint or quart containers.

I never salt stock until I use it in a recipe. If you do use canned broth, taste the dish first before adding any salt.

Browning the bones in a hot oven before boiling will give a richer flavor and color, and is done mostly with beef and lamb stocks.

Stock, fish: Save all fish bones and shrimp and lobster shells, and ask at the fish store for any heads. Freeze until you have about 3 pounds. Cover with cold water, add a celery stalk, a quartered onion, and a few peppercorns, and bring to a boil. Skim off any foam that rises and simmer for an hour. Strain the stock through a fine-meshed sieve, discard the solids, and freeze the broth in 1-cup plastic containers. A good quick stock is bottled clam broth diluted with an equal amount of water.

Stock, vegetable: Brown 2 cups each chopped onions, carrots, and celery in 2 tablespoons canola or pure olive oil over medium heat, then cover with 2 quarts of water. Add 2 cups potato peelings and some garlic and bring to a boil. Simmer for an hour, then strain and freeze in 1-cup plastic containers.

Butter: I use unsalted butter for the best flavor. When making pies and biscuits, I mix butter and vegetable shortening, butter for flavor, shortening for flakiness. To maintain its freshness, keep butter in the freezer, wrapped in plastic wrap, and pull out only what you need for a few days.

Buttermilk: If you have no fresh buttermilk on hand, substitute sour milk (1 cup milk curdled with 1 tablespoon lemon juice or vinegar) or yogurt or sour cream thinned with water. Dried buttermilk is handy for baking as you only use what you need. This buttermilk powder keeps well in the refrigerator and can be substituted for each cup of fresh buttermilk by mixing 3 tablespoons of the powder in with the dry ingredients and using 1 cup of water.

Canned tomatoes: Look for brands sold in lined cans for best flavor. I like Dei Fratelli, Redpack, and Muir Glen best. I tend to freeze my summer tomatoes, because I am too busy making jam!

Cheese: Sharp or extra-sharp Vermont Cheddar made by Cabot, Grafton, Seward, or Shelburne Farms has good flavor and melting ability. Sage cheese is also available. Freshly grated Parmesan from Italy has a nutty, mild flavor. If you like a sharper cheese flavor, try grating a hard provolone or pecorino Romano. Swiss cheese, either Gruyère or Emmenthaler, melts well and has a smooth, nutty flavor. Feta is a sharply flavored Greek cheese that comes stored in brine, and will keep well left in its brine. To store, wrap all cheeses well and refrigerate.

Cider: Fresh apple cider is available most of the year. When boiled down to a syrup, it is known as "boiled cider." Cooked further, it becomes cider jelly. Refrigerate all of these products after opening.

When fresh cider starts to ferment, it becomes "hard." The alcohol content of hard cider varies from 5 to 7 percent. It is usually sold in six-packs next to the beer.

Cocoa: Unsweetened cocoa is made richer tasting through a Dutch process, which treats cocoa with alkali to neutralize the natural acids. Look for Droste or Callebaut brands for the finest flavors. Sift to remove lumps.

Cornmeal: Use stone-ground white or yellow cornmeal and store it in the freezer to keep it at its freshest.

Crème fraîche: This is naturally thickened cream made by mixing 1 tablespoon buttermilk, yogurt, or sour cream with 1 cup heavy cream and allowing it to stand in a warm place 6 to 24 hours until thickened. It can be boiled, unlike heavy cream, which curdles. This was called "clabbered cream" in the old days. It will keep in the refrigerator for up to three weeks.

Dried beans: Soldier, Jacob's Cattle, Great Northern, and Yellow Eye are just some of the many varieties of dried beans available. Either soak beans overnight in cold water to cover or use the quick method: Cover the beans with water, bring to a boil, cover, and let sit for 1 hour, then continue with the recipe. Keep all beans tightly covered.

Dried chestnuts: These are very handy to have around, because fresh chestnuts are not available after the holidays. The chestnuts need to be soaked in boiling water, then left overnight to reconstitute. They have a light smoky flavor. Chestnuts are available in Chinese and Italian groceries, and health food stores. Store in a tightly covered jar.

Dried mushrooms: Look for dried Chilean mushrooms in the health food store or use dried shiitakes, chanterelles, or porcinis. These must be soaked before using to soften and then rinsed well to remove grit. Store in a tightly covered jar.

Eggs: All the recipes in this book call for large eggs. For substituting purposes, if you have eggs of another size, it's helpful to know that 5 large eggs equals 1 cup.

Flour: Use unbleached all-purpose flour unless a recipe calls for cake flour. If you have no cake flour, substitute by spooning 2 tablespoons cornstarch into a 1-cup measure and filling it with all-purpose flour.

Use stone-ground whole-wheat and rye flours and store them in the freezer. Measure flours by spooning them lightly into a measuring cup and leveling it off. Don't pack flour in or shake the cup to settle the flour, or you will be adding too much of it to your baked goods and they will be heavy and disappointing. I sift only cake flour; all other flours get stirred together with the other dry ingredients.

Ham, bacon, hocks, and salt pork: Vermont produces delicious smoked maple-cured hams and bacon. Smoked hocks are inexpensive and impart good flavor to soup and bean dishes. Look for salt pork that is more meat than fat. I always freeze these pork products if I don't plan on using them within a week.

Herbs: Fresh herbs are superior in taste to dried, but some recipes require dried. For substitution, use 1 teaspoon dried herbs for 1 tablespoon fresh. Use herbs carefully, as they can overpower delicate flavors. Think of them as supporting actors. Dried herbs should be stored tightly closed and discarded when they have lost their fragrance. Happily, supermarkets are carrying fresh herbs year-round for those of us without winter window box gardens. Some fresh herbs, like basil, can be frozen for winter use or be finely chopped, covered in olive oil, and refrigerated.

Maple syrup and sugar: Only pure Vermont maple syrup will do, but for cooking and baking, use dark amber or grade B for the best flavor. For great maple taste, if you can find maple sugar, use it in place of brown sugar. Keep the syrup refrigerated after opening and the sugar in a tightly closed container.

Old-fashioned rolled oats: Do not use quick-cooking or instant oats. The old-fashioned rolled oat provides texture and flavor to cakes, biscuits, and cookies. The other types get gummy.

Polenta: Cooked cornmeal with an Italian name, this grain goes well with most gravies and is a traditional country food. It was common in the early days to have cornmeal mush and milk for supper. To make, gradually sprinkle ½ cup cornmeal into 3 cups boiling water, whisking continuously to prevent lumps. Cook until very thick, about 10 minutes. Add salt, butter, and cheese to taste. Use as is or pour into a pie plate and cool. The polenta can then be sliced and fried in butter or oil.

Salt : kosher, canning, or sea : There is an old saying when the food is too salty, "Oh, the cook must be in love!" Using kosher salt helps prevent oversalting because the crystals are larger than regular table salt, and kosher salt has great ability to cling to food. I find myself using it most of the time when cooking. Canning salt is very pure and is used when pickling to retain the best color in the brine. Sea salt is best in flavor, rich in minerals, and available in fine and coarse crystals. I use fine sea salt in baking and on the table.

Semolina : A grain of hard durum wheat that is ground like cornmeal, semolina gives flavor and texture to breads, and is used to absorb fruit juices in pies. Pasta is made from semolina flour and both are available in Italian markets and health food stores. Store in the freezer.

Sugar : Unless another sugar is called for, use granulated sugar. Brown sugar, light or dark, is always firmly packed into the cup when measuring.

Vanilla : Pure vanilla extract is worth its price because the taste is wonderful and a small amount delivers a large effect. To retain the most flavor, add extract at the end of cooking.

Vanilla beans can be cooked and reused several times and can flavor a jar of sugar even when they look all tired out. Just wipe the beans dry and wrap in plastic wrap. After two or three times more use, dry the beans and add them to a jar of sugar. After a week or so the sugar will be perfumed with vanilla.

Yeast : Dry yeast is a great invention because it lasts for a long time when stored in the freezer. It is less expensive to buy yeast in bulk if you do a great deal of baking. Always proof the yeast in warm water if you have any doubts about its freshness. Yeast can be killed by water that is too hot, so keep the temperature around 110° to 115°F.

Some Friendly Advice on Kitchen Skills

Our kitchens are loaded with toaster ovens, microwaves, bread machines, food processors, espresso machines, and many other gadgets. Our stores are filled with instant this and already made that. Statistics tell us that we eat out more than 38 percent of the time. So who's cooking, and why do we need all this stuff?

I meet people all the time who are very interested in cooking, but seem to think equipment is what makes a good cook. Not so! No one needs more plastic machinery to separate us from our food. To smell, touch, and taste food is to start to appreciate how to cook it well. Now, please don't think that I am cooking over a wood fire here. I love my instant thermometer and KitchenAid mixer with a passion. They make some tasks much easier. But you can keep that microwave! I love the smell, the sizzle, and the look of food cooking right in front of me where I can use my knowledge to judge when to turn it over, when to add the sauce, whether it needs something to complement the flavor, and everything else that goes into putting a good meal on the table.

I encourage you to learn the basics. Develop those fast-disappearing skills of our grandparents. Know that a stew is a stew in any language, whether flavored with ginger and cilantro, chiles, or thyme leaves and a bay leaf. Learn to distinguish cuts of meat, when fish is fresh, when to use canned tomatoes instead of fresh. Learn to feel the texture of pie crust, when bread dough is elastic, the temperature of a custard to prevent curdling. *Don't* be afraid to experiment with flavors and *do* pay attention to measuring when baking. An aside on measuring: Many people will say that their grandmothers never measured anything. Not true! They may have held salt in their hand or used a teacup for flour, but it was always the same hand and the same teacup.

Beef, Lamb, and Pork
Supper Dishes

THE TASTIEST BEEF I have ever eaten is raised by Paddy Martin at Spring Lake Ranch, twenty minutes from my home in Vermont. I don't know if it is the beautiful surroundings or the TLC that Paddy lavishes on that herd, but the resulting meat is delicious.

Spring Lake Ranch is a therapeutic community for mentally and emotionally ill adults set high up in the mountains of Shrewsbury, Vermont. For the past six years I worked there as the chef. One year the town was invited to a big Labor Day supper at the ranch, where we barbecued four enormous steamship rounds of beef that Paddy and I had marinated for several days. Folks stayed up all night turning the spit over the wood fire to roast the meat. The neighbors brought side dishes, salads, and desserts and we would share a memorable end to summer.

About fifteen years ago, people interested in sustaining the local farm economy promoted native Vermont beef as an alternative to Western beef. Not enough production or interest or both perhaps let this idea drift away. Recently, however, more and more people are looking for hormone-free, naturally, and organically raised beef and the Vermont Agricultural Department is again encouraging more local beef production.

In the 1830s most of Vermont was cleared of trees to provide pasture for sheep. But the wool market started to die before the Civil War as the lure of open land began to draw farmers to the West. Reports of the Vermont Board of Agriculture of 1877 show farmers and the Agriculture Department discussing the turn from sheep farming to dairying. The discussion continues because today we see a decline in dairy farming and sheep are returning once more to our hillsides as farmers respond to an increase in consumer interest in lamb. The influences of French, Italian, and Middle Eastern cuisines have shown how delicious lamb can be. Some people have old prejudices about the gaminess of the flavor of the older lamb that was previously marketed. Lamb raised today is younger and lighter in flavor. In cooking lamb, I recommend trimming as much fat off the meat as possible. Lamb fat contributes to that muttony flavor some people find objectionable.

Lamb is rarely found at community suppers except for an occasional Irish stew on St. Patrick's Day. As the yield from a lamb is not as great as from a cow or pig, the meat is often served on special occasions. The Biddles, who raise lambs in nearby Shrewsbury, served a gorgeous dandelion-stuffed lamb for their daughter's wedding. Lamb can be fancy or homey and this chapter offers a number of ways to enjoy the succulence of this meat.

The pig has proved truly indispensable to country people, as they could use all of it, except, as the saying went, the "oink!" There was not a cellar without a barrel of salt pork and to this day Vermont has some of the most delicious smoked hams available. An old folk saying, found in the *Green Mountain Whittlin's* collection of Vermont folklore, says "Butcher a pig in the full of the moon and when you fry it up it will be nice and full."

Pork is a versatile meat, eaten fresh, smoked, and cured. Because today's pork is leaner and raised under more sanitary conditions with improved feeding techniques, it is unnecessary to cook the meat as long as it was in the past. A temperature of 160°F is hot enough to ensure safe eating, and any higher than that and you will end up with dried-out meat.

Roast pork suppers are very common in the colder months. One local church runs a monthly dinner to raise money to pay its fuel bill. And the idea of a potluck supper without a crock of baked beans seasoned with salt pork, ham hocks, or streaky bacon is unimaginable.

Much of the family budget is spent on meat and yet so few people are knowledgeable about the different cuts, the appropriate cooking methods, and getting the most for your money. The majority of meat is bought in sterile packages from the supermarket, with little consumer confidence in and connection to the people involved in the raising and butchering of the meat people eat.

Getting your money's worth is a true New England virtue, and being a smart consumer can save you from buying the wrong cut or type of meat. There are books available in most public libraries (see Bibliography) that can teach you everything you need to know about selecting, buying, cutting, storing, and freezing meat. The recipes in this chapter will help you discover some very good eating beyond the usual hamburgers and steak, and in the process expand your cooking repertoire to include wonderfully flavorful, old-fashioned dishes that will taste brand new to many.

COUNTRY TIPS AND TALES

Notice in a recent *Rutland Herald*:

Roast Beef Supper
Belmont, roast beef supper served family style.
I.O.O.F. Hall, 5:30 P.M
Benefit Mount Holly Boy Scouts

Herb-Crusted Roast Beef

MAKES 8 TO 10 SERVINGS

Roast beef, mashed potatoes, and gravy—could any meal be more American? Standing in line for the annual roast beef supper in the East Poultney church, we gabbed with our neighbors about local politics. This church sits on the quintessential New England town green surrounded by houses built in the last century. In the little historical museum was a notice from the 1800s advertising a town supper that promised "foot warmers to keep the ladies warm."

I developed this savory version to give additional interest to an inexpensive cut of meat. Bottom round roast makes a juicy, flavorful, and much less fatty roast than does prime rib. Top round or eye round are other cuts of meat you can use. Those of you who like well-done meat are out of luck here. Because of its leanness, bottom round gets tough if cooked beyond the medium stage.

Here is an instance when the use of dried herbs instead of fresh is important. I let the herbs flavor the meat overnight.

One 5-pound bottom round roast

3 large cloves garlic, peeled

1 tablespoon kosher salt

1 tablespoon black peppercorns

1 teaspoon dried rosemary

1 teaspoon dried marjoram

FOR GRAVY (OPTIONAL)

2 cups beef stock (page 2)

2 tablespoons all-purpose flour

¼ cup water

Place the meat in a roasting pan and pat it dry with paper towels. In a mortar, blender, or mini food processor, crush the garlic with the salt, peppercorns, rosemary, and marjoram into a paste. Rub this mixture into the meat on all sides. Cover with plastic wrap and refrigerate overnight to let the flavors penetrate the meat.

Several hours before serving, remove the meat from the refrigerator, unwrap it, and let it come to room temperature for 1 hour. Preheat the oven to 425°F. Roast the meat for 30 minutes, then reduce the oven temperature to 350°F. Roast the meat until the internal temperature reads 120°F when you insert an instant meat thermometer into the thickest part of the meat, about 1 hour longer. If you prefer the meat to be less rare, cook it to 130°F. Remove the roast to a carving board and let it rest for 15 minutes. Slice the meat thinly across the grain and place the slices on a serving platter.

Degrease the pan juices and drizzle over the meat. Or if you absolutely must have gravy, stir the beef stock into the degreased pan juices, scrape up all the browned bits from the pan, and pour into a small saucepan. Stir the flour into the water until smooth. Bring the gravy to a boil and whisk in the flour slurry. Cook over low heat for 5 minutes and taste for seasoning.

COUNTRY TIPS AND TALES

Make extra gravy for hot roast beef sandwiches on Buttermilk Bread (page 116) for supper the next evening.

Yankee Pot Roast

Straightforward and hearty is this pot roast, perfect for serving after a day of skiing or snowshoeing. Use a piece of chuck roast or shoulder roast for the best flavor. Some people, like my mother, prefer to use a fresh brisket, but this cut is often difficult to find in Vermont. I like the gelatinous texture and rich flavor of the chuck roast. You can cook this in the oven as well as on top of the stove.

One 2- to 2½-pound chuck roast
1 tablespoon vegetable oil
1 cup coarsely chopped onions
1 pound carrots, cut into 1-inch-thick slices
1 pound turnips, peeled and cut into 1-inch pieces
3 stalks celery, cut into 1-inch-thick slices
1 teaspoon dried thyme leaves
1 bay leaf
2 teaspoons salt
½ teaspoon freshly ground black pepper
4 cups water

FOR THICKENING THE GRAVY (OPTIONAL)
3 tablespoons all-purpose flour
½ cup cold water

Preheat the oven to 350°F. Pat the meat dry with paper towels. Heat the oil in a heavy-bottomed ovenproof pot over medium-high heat and brown the meat on all sides. Add the remaining ingredients, bring to a boil, cover, and place in the oven.

Cook for 1 hour, turn the meat over, cover, and cook until the meat is tender when pierced with a fork, about 1 hour more.

Remove the meat from the liquid and cover it with a sheet of aluminum foil to keep warm. Skim all the fat from the surface of the gravy and taste for seasoning. If you want a thick gravy, mix the flour and water together until smooth. Bring the gravy to a boil and whisk in the flour slurry. Reduce to low heat, cook for several minutes, and season to taste. Slice the meat, place the slices on a serving platter, and spoon the vegetables and gravy over the meat.

COUNTRY TIPS AND TALES

A poem about gravies:

The spirit of each dish, and ZEST of all
Is what ingenious cooks the relish call
For though the market sends in loads of food
They are all tasteless 'til that makes them good.
—King, *The Art of Cookery*, London, 1709

Vermont Boiled Dinner

Simplicity is a one-pot meal and this classic dinner has everything in it. Most St. Patrick's Day suppers feature this dish, but it is a standard in the Vermont repertoire. Corning, or curing beef in a salt brine, was the only way to keep meat from spoiling in days past. Huge crocks seen today at antique shows stored the meats in the cold cellar. Tradition demands side dishes of mustard, horseradish, and pickled beets to be served with the meat, and a pitcher of cider vinegar to douse the cabbage.

Corned beef brisket releases a good amount of fat, so degrease the broth carefully. Most stores carry brands that have a packet of spices included with the meat. If no spices are included, use 2 tablespoons of pickling spices. You should have leftover broth—save it to make a delicious bean soup. Remember, real Yankees are real frugal.

4 quarts water
One 4- to 5-pound corned beef brisket with spices
1 pound carrots, cut into 2-inch chunks
1 large onion, cut into 8 wedges
1 medium-size head green cabbage, cut into 8 wedges
20 small red-skinned potatoes, scrubbed

Bring the water to a boil in a large, heavy-bottomed pot or Dutch oven over medium heat and add the meat. Let the water return to a boil, skim off any foam that rises to the top, add the spices, and cover the pot. Reduce the heat to medium-low and cook gently until the meat is tender when pierced with a fork; this can take up to 3 hours.

Remove the meat from the liquid and cover it with a sheet of aluminum foil to keep warm. Skim all the fat from the surface of the broth. Add the carrots and onions to the broth and continue to cook for 20 minutes. Add the cabbage and potatoes and cook until the potatoes and carrots are tender, about 20 minutes more.

Slice the meat across the grain and place the slices in a deep platter. Spoon the vegetables around the meat and moisten the meat and vegetables with some broth. Serve with piquant condiments.

Old-fashioned Beef Stew

MAKES 6 TO 8 SERVINGS

Stew always tastes best the next day, and can be multiplied easily to feed a crowd. Unlike many braised dishes, the meat is not browned before stewing, an example of plain country cooking. This hearty, one-pot meal will warm up everybody when the temperature in February is 20°F below zero and dropping! A big green salad with shredded cabbage and some crusty bread rounds out this supper.

2 pounds chuck or beef shoulder, cut into 2-inch cubes

2 cups coarsely chopped onions

1 bay leaf

1 teaspoon dried thyme leaves

2 teaspoons salt

½ teaspoon freshly ground black pepper

4 cups water

1 pound carrots, cut into 2-inch chunks

1 pound boiling potatoes, peeled and cut into 2-inch chunks

2 tablespoons unsalted butter

3 tablespoons all-purpose flour

Place the meat, onions, bay leaf, thyme, salt, pepper, and water in a large, heavy-bottomed pot. Bring to a boil over high heat, skim off the foam that rises to the surface, cover, reduce the heat to medium-low, and cook until the meat is almost tender, about 1 hour. Add the carrots and potatoes, cover, and cook 20 minutes longer.

In a small pot, heat the butter over medium heat until it is sizzling, and whisk in the flour until the mixture is thickened. Cook for 2 minutes, stirring often. Raise the heat under the stew to medium, cook until boiling, and stir in the flour mixture. Boil for 3 minutes, stirring constantly, then reduce the heat to medium-low and cook, uncovered, for 15 minutes. Remove from the heat, let the stew sit for 10 minutes, and skim any fat. Adjust the seasoning before serving.

Ragout of Beef

Ragout means a thick, savory stew and this delicious version can be varied by using wine or adding mushrooms. There are many variations of this stew served at French-Canadian and Italian tables, proving that a stew is a stew is a stew.

If you haven't got homemade beef stock and use canned broth instead, be careful when adding salt. Look for brands of canned tomatoes that are packed in lined cans; the fresh flavor is retained and the tomatoes do not pick up that tinny taste. Sometimes I like to add a package of thawed petite peas to the ragout before serving.

1 tablespoon olive oil

2 pounds chuck roast or beef shoulder, cut into 2-inch cubes

1 cup slivered onions

2 cloves garlic, peeled and minced

1 teaspoon dried rosemary

3 tablespoons all-purpose flour

½ teaspoon salt

¼ teaspoon freshly ground black pepper

2 cups canned diced tomatoes

1 cup beef stock (page 2)

1 tablespoon minced fresh parsley leaves

Heat the oil in a large, heavy-bottomed pot over medium heat. Pat the meat dry and brown it in the oil on all sides in several batches. Return all the meat to the pot along with the onions, garlic, and rosemary and cook together, stirring occasionally, for 3 minutes. Sprinkle with the flour, salt, and pepper and cook 3 minutes longer, stirring often. Add the tomatoes and stock and stir well, scraping up all the browned bits from the bottom of the pot. Bring to a boil, reduce the heat to medium-low, cover, and cook until the meat is tender when pierced with a fork, 1 to 1½ hours.

Tilt the pot and skim off all the fat. Sprinkle with the parsley and serve over noodles or polenta.

Boeuf à la Mode

My mother-in-law, Mary Cousineau, makes this old-fashioned potted meat the way she learned from her mother-in-law. It is redolent of cloves and cinnamon, which surely descended from the French use of *quatre épices*. The large amount of onions and garlic provides the moisture as well as the flavoring for this aromatic dish.

One 2½- to 3-pound chuck or shoulder roast
1 teaspoon salt
½ teaspoon ground cinnamon
½ teaspoon ground cloves
¼ teaspoon freshly ground black pepper
4 cups slivered onions
4 cloves garlic, peeled and minced
1 tablespoon minced fresh parsley leaves

Preheat the oven to 400°F. Combine the salt, cinnamon, cloves, and pepper and rub the mixture on the meat. Place half of the onions and garlic in the bottom of a baking pan and set the roast on top. Layer the remaining onions and garlic on the meat. Cover the pan tightly with aluminum foil and cook until the meat is tender when pierced with a fork, 2 to 3 hours.

Slice the meat and place the slices in a serving dish. Skim any fat from the pan juices, spoon them over the meat, sprinkle with the parsley, and serve.

COUNTRY TIPS AND TALES

Cow Appreciation Day
Woodstock, Billings Farm & Museum provides
information, competitions, and contest.
10 A.M.—5 P.M.

Beef and Cheddar Pie

MAKES 6 TO 8 SERVINGS

If maple syrup is Vermont's liquid gold, then Cheddar is our gold bar. I like to use the sharpest Cheddar, such as Cabot's Hunters, for this double-crusted pie. This is a good dish to take to a covered-dish or potluck supper and it can be made with many variations. Try using a jalapeño jack cheese and some cumin for a Tex-Mex version.

FOR THE FILLING

1½ pounds lean ground beef

1 cup finely chopped onions

½ teaspoon dry mustard

½ teaspoon salt

¼ teaspoon freshly ground black pepper

¼ cup all-purpose flour

1½ cups shredded extra-sharp Cheddar cheese

FOR THE BISCUIT DOUGH

¾ cup all-purpose flour

¾ teaspoon baking powder

1 teaspoon salt

2 tablespoons vegetable shortening

¼ cup plus 1 tablespoon milk

Preheat the oven to 425°F. To make the filling, cook the beef with the onions in a large skillet over medium heat, stirring occasionally, until the beef loses all its pinkness, 5 to 6 minutes. Sprinkle with the mustard, salt, pepper, and flour and cook 3 to 4 minutes longer, stirring the mixture well. Stir in the Cheddar and set aside to cool.

To make the dough, place the flour, baking powder, and salt in a bowl and stir to combine. Cut in the shortening with a pastry blender or two knives or rub it in with your fingers until the mixture resembles oatmeal. Stir in the ¼ cup milk with a fork just until the dough holds together. Turn the dough out onto a lightly floured worktable and knead 10 to 12 times. Cut the dough in half and roll one half into a 12-inch circle. Fit it into a 9-inch pie plate and spoon in the filling. Roll out the remaining dough into a 12-inch circle and drape over the filling. Trim off the excess dough and crimp the edges to seal. Cut several steam vents in the top crust and brush it with the remaining table-spoon of milk.

Bake until the pie is golden brown, 20 to 30 minutes. Let rest for 10 minutes for easier slicing.

Flank Steak Sandwiches

MAKES 4 TO 6 SERVINGS

Life in the country can get hectic. Not only are some folks caring for gardens and livestock, but they are also working full time, and driving the kids to music and ballet lessons. Often all one has time for is a supper of soup and sandwiches. This hearty sandwich absolutely requires a good, crusty hero roll. Pair with a bowl of Italian Green Bean Soup (page 106) and you have a truly satisfying meal.

One 1½-pound piece flank steak
Salt and freshly ground black pepper to taste
¼ cup (½ stick) unsalted butter, at room temperature
1 tablespoon minced shallots
1 teaspoon minced garlic
2 tablespoons minced fresh parsley leaves
1 tablespoon grainy prepared mustard
6 crusty rolls

Season the meat with salt and pepper. Heat the grill or a ridged cast-iron griddle or frying pan over high heat and cook the steak for 5 minutes on each side. If you like rare meat, the internal temperature should read 120°F when you insert an instant meat thermometer into the thickest part of the steak. (Another indication that the meat has cooked to rare is that the juices start coming to the surface of the meat.) Remove the meat to a cutting board and let it rest for 10 minutes.

Mash the butter together with the shallots, garlic, parsley, and mustard in a small bowl. Cut each roll in half lengthwise and spread the butter mixture on the cut sides of the rolls. Slice the steak on the diagonal into very thin slices across the grain of the meat. Place the meat on the rolls and serve.

Braised Short Ribs in Cider

MAKES 4 TO 6 SERVINGS

Short ribs are full of flavor, but they need long simmering to tenderize the meat. Use a hard, dry cider like Cider Jack and Woodchuck draft, made in Vermont and found in the beer section in the supermarket, to braise the meat. Invite only those friends who like to pick up the ribs and nibble on the bones. Use a covered pot or Dutch oven large enough to hold the ribs in a single layer. Serve this with mashed potatoes, Three-Root Mash (page 144), or polenta.

1 tablespoon vegetable oil

3½ pounds short ribs

1½ cups sliced onions

3 tablespoons all-purpose flour

1 teaspoon dried thyme leaves

2 teaspoons salt

¼ teaspoon freshly ground black pepper

3 cups (two 12-ounce bottles) dry cider

In a large, heavy-bottomed pot, heat the oil over medium heat and brown the ribs, a few at a time, on all sides. Set them aside and discard all but 1 tablespoon of the fat from the pan. Add the onions and cook them over low heat, stirring occasionally, until they begin to brown, about 20 minutes.

Return the meat to the pan along with any accumulated juices, sprinkle with the flour, thyme, salt, and pepper, and stir with the onions. Cook for several minutes, add the cider, raise the heat to medium-high, and bring the liquid to a boil. Reduce the heat to medium-low, cover, and cook gently until the meat is tender when pierced with a fork, about 2 hours.

Tilt the pot and carefully skim the fat from the gravy. Adjust the seasoning and serve.

Corned Beef Hash

MAKES 4 SERVINGS

Homemade hash is a treat and it is really worth saving some of the corned beef from the Vermont Boiled Dinner (page 14) especially for it. The difference between homemade and canned hash is amazing, like the difference between frozen fish sticks and homemade fish cakes. If you decide to cook eggs with the hash, a cast-iron skillet works best.

    1 tablespoon vegetable oil
    1 cup diced onions
    2 cups peeled and cubed potatoes, cooked in water to cover until tender,
        then drained
    2 cups coarsely chopped cooked corned beef
    ⅓ cup heavy cream
    ¼ teaspoon salt
    ¼ teaspoon freshly ground black pepper
    4 large eggs (optional)

Heat the oil in a large, heavy-bottomed skillet over medium heat and cook the onions, stirring often, until they begin to brown, about 10 minutes. Add the potatoes and meat and cook for 20 minutes, scraping up the bits of browned meat and potato that stick to the pan. Continue to cook until the mixture is browned, drizzle on the cream, and heat through. Season with salt and pepper.

Serve as is or make it with eggs. To do this, preheat the oven to 400°F. Make four depressions in the hash and crack an egg into each one. Sprinkle the eggs with salt and pepper, put the pan into the oven, and bake until the eggs are set, about 10 minutes.

COUNTRY TIPS AND TALES

Some cooks add chopped cooked beets to their hash
and call it "red flannel hash."

Roasted Leg of Lamb

MAKES 8 TO 10 SERVINGS

A whole leg of lamb studded with garlic and rosemary and roasted until it is medium rare is one of my favorite meats to serve friends and family. Roasting on the bone makes the meat especially succulent.

One 7- to 9-pound leg of lamb
3 cloves garlic, each peeled and cut into 4 slivers
12 small sprigs fresh rosemary or 2 teaspoons dried
2 tablespoons pure olive oil
1 tablespoon kosher salt
½ teaspoon freshly ground black pepper

Preheat the oven to 350°F. With a sharp knife, remove all visible fat from the outside of the lamb. Make six slits into the meat on each side and stuff them with the garlic slivers and rosemary. Rub the oil into the meat and sprinkle with the salt and pepper.

Place the meat on a rack in a roasting pan. Roast until an instant meat thermometer inserted in the thickest part of the meat reads 125°F, about 1½ hours. Remove the lamb to a cutting board and let rest for 15 minutes before carving into thin slices. Skim any fat off the pan juices and drizzle them over the meat.

COUNTRY TIPS AND TALES

Always let meat sit at room temperature for an hour before roasting it or you will need to increase the cooking time by about half an hour.

Welsh Lamb with Cloves

This recipe comes from Jan Edwards, who is researching her genealogy. She grew up in the slate mining area of western Vermont in a community of Welsh descendants.

Please, please throw away that jar of sickeningly sweet Day-Glo-green mint jelly sitting in the back of your refrigerator, and try some of my friend Michael Wells's real mint sauce. He was a child in England during World War II when he could only dream about this sauce.

FOR FRESH MINT SAUCE (OPTIONAL)

⅔ cup cider vinegar

3 tablespoons sugar

1 cup packed finely chopped fresh mint leaves

FOR THE LAMB

One 7- to 9-pound leg of lamb

36 whole cloves

Salt and freshly ground black pepper to taste

To make the sauce, place the vinegar and sugar in a small, nonreactive saucepan over medium heat and bring to a boil. Pour over the mint in a small bowl and let the sauce sit several hours before serving.

Preheat the oven to 350°F. Remove all visible fat from the outside of the lamb and stud it all over with the cloves. Sprinkle the lamb with the salt and pepper and place on a rack in a roasting pan. Roast the lamb until an instant meat thermometer inserted into the thickest part of the meat reads 125°F, about 1½ hours. Remove from the oven and let rest for 15 minutes. Remove the cloves before carving the meat. Serve the mint sauce on the side.

COUNTRY TIPS AND TALES

Too often cooks leave on the lamb fat, which gives the meat a muttony taste. Remove all the fat and you will be delighted with the lightness of the lamb flavor.

Stark Biddle's Drunken Lamb

In total contrast to the roast leg of lamb, this leg cooks for hours, until it is so soft it can be eaten with a spoon! It is an old French recipe adapted by Stark to show off the beautiful lamb he and his wife, Ludie, raise on their farm, nestled on a hillside in North Shrewsbury.

6 large onions, peeled and quartered

6 carrots, quartered

6 bay leaves

1 bunch fresh thyme

One 7- to 9-pound leg of lamb, all visible fat removed

4 cloves garlic, peeled and cut into slivers

1 tablespoon salt

2 bottles dry white wine

6 large boiling potatoes, peeled and quartered

5 large, ripe tomatoes, peeled, seeded, and coarsely chopped, or 4 cups canned
   diced tomatoes

Freshly ground black pepper to taste

Preheat the oven to 425°F. Place the onions, carrots, bay leaves, and thyme in a large Dutch oven or deep roasting pan big enough to hold the lamb leg. Make slits in the lamb with a sharp knife and stuff the garlic slivers into them. Lay the lamb on the bed of vegetables and sprinkle with the salt. Roast, uncovered, for 1 hour. Add the wine and reduce the temperature to 325°F. Cover and cook for 2½ hours. Add the potatoes and tomatoes and cook 45 minutes to 1 hour more. The meat should be falling off the bone and completely tender. Remove from the oven. Remove the bones, bay leaves, and thyme branches and skim the fat from the sauce. Adjust the seasoning and add pepper.

Braised Lamb Shoulder

This cut of meat is often neglected, which is too bad because it makes for many a delicious meal. Stuffed with a spinach-pancetta mixture, rolled, tied and then roasted, it becomes an elegant dinner. Even easier is to braise it slowly with herbs and garlic. Serve it with Scalloped Potatoes (see page 142) and sautéed fennel. Equally good winter or summer.

One 3- to 3½-pound lamb shoulder, boned and tied
    (your butcher can do this for you)
2 tablespoons pure olive oil
4 cloves garlic, peeled
1 teaspoon dried thyme leaves
½ teaspoon crushed anise or fennel seeds
½ teaspoon dried marjoram
½ teaspoon dried rosemary
1 teaspoon salt
¼ teaspoon freshly ground black pepper
2 strips orange rind, 1 × 2 inches each
2 cups lamb or beef stock (page 2)
2 tablespoons minced fresh parsley leaves

Preheat the oven to 350°F. Wipe the lamb dry with paper towels. Heat the oil in an ovenproof casserole or Dutch oven over medium heat and brown the lamb on all sides. Add the remaining ingredients except the parsley and bring to a boil. Cover tightly and place the casserole in the oven. After 45 minutes, turn the lamb over, cover again, and braise until the meat is tender when pierced with a fork, 30 to 40 minutes.

Remove the meat from the sauce and cut off the strings. Slice the meat and overlap the slices on a platter. Cover them with a sheet of aluminum foil to keep warm. Skim all the fat from the sauce and adjust the seasoning. Stir in the parsley, spoon some sauce over the lamb, and pass the remainder separately.

Irish Lamb Stew

MAKES 4 TO 6 SERVINGS

My co-author of *Tomato Imperative!*, Sharon Nimtz, introduced me to lovage. A big, handsome herb, lovage is best planted out of the way, as it can take over. I dry some to use in the winter. It has a strong celery flavor and a few leaves in this stew are very tasty. This may be the dish to offer next St. Patrick's Day for a change from corned beef and cabbage.

2 pounds lamb shoulder or stew meat, cut into 1-inch chunks

1 pound carrots, cut into 1-inch chunks

1 cup coarsely chopped onions

4 cups water

¼ cup Irish whiskey

1 tablespoon salt

½ teaspoon dried thyme leaves

¼ teaspoon freshly ground black pepper

A few dried lovage leaves or fresh celery leaves

2 cups 1-inch chunks unpeeled boiling potatoes

3 tablespoons all-purpose flour mixed with ½ cup water until smooth

2 tablespoons minced fresh parsley leaves

continued

Place the lamb, carrots, and onions in a 4-quart pot. Add the water and whiskey and bring to a boil over medium heat, skimming off any foam. Add the salt, thyme, pepper, and lovage. Stir well, cover, reduce the heat to medium-low, and cook until the meat is tender when pierced with a fork, about 1 hour Add the potatoes, cover, and cook for 30 minutes. Skim off any fat from the sauce. Restir the flour-and-water mixture and stir into the stew, cooking until the sauce thickens. Adjust the seasoning and sprinkle with the parsley leaves before serving.

Lamb Pot Pie with Kohlrabi

MAKES 6 TO 8 SERVINGS

Kohlrabi is great fun to grow, as it looks like a flying saucer. Peeled and cut raw into salads, its sweet cabbage flavor and crunch will make folks ask, "What is this vegetable?"

This Hungarian version of pot pie was inspired by a delicious goulash served last winter at a friend's house down the road in West Rutland.

FOR THE FILLING

2 pounds lamb shoulder or stew meat, cut into 1-inch cubes

2 tablespoons vegetable oil

4 cloves garlic, peeled and minced

2 tablespoons all-purpose flour

1 tablespoon sweet Hungarian paprika

1 teaspoon salt

¼ teaspoon freshly ground black pepper

2 cups lamb or beef stock (page 2)

2 cups 1-inch cubes peeled kohlrabi

FOR THE CARAWAY BISCUIT DOUGH

1½ cups all-purpose flour

½ cup rye flour (available in health food stores)

1 tablespoon sugar

2 teaspoons baking powder

1 teaspoon baking soda

½ teaspoon salt

⅛ teaspoon freshly ground black pepper

1 tablespoon crushed caraway seeds

¼ cup (½ stick) unsalted butter

1¼ cups buttermilk

Sour cream

To make the filling, pat the meat dry with paper towels. Heat the oil in a large, heavy-bottomed skillet over medium-high heat and brown the meat on all sides in several batches. Return all the meat to the skillet and add the garlic, flour, paprika, salt, and pepper. Stir together and cook for 1 minute. Add the stock, and bring to a boil over medium heat. Add the kohlrabi, reduce the heat to medium-low, and cook until the kohlrabi is almost tender, about 12 minutes. Remove from the heat and skim off any fat from the sauce. Spoon the mixture into a medium-size baking dish.

Preheat the oven to 400°F. To make the crust, stir the flours, sugar, baking powder and soda, salt, pepper, and caraway seeds together in a medium-size bowl. Cut in the butter with a pastry blender or two knives or rub it in with your fingers until the mixture resembles oatmeal. Stir in the buttermilk with a fork just until a soft dough is formed. Drop the dough by rounded tablespoonfuls on top of the lamb mixture, leaving space between each spoonful. Bake until the dough is golden brown and the sauce is bubbling, 40 to 50 minutes. Pass the sour cream for each person to spoon on their pie.

Shepherd's Pie
with Turnip-Potato Crust

MAKES 4 TO 6 SERVINGS

A soothing winter supper casserole made with cooked lamb and covered with a lid of mashed "taties and neeps." Try Yukon Golds;
their yellow flesh tastes buttery and sweet. The little purple-and-white
turnips are the ones to use, but a rutabaga would be a fine substitute. If
you use a 10-inch ovenproof skillet to sauté the vegetables, you can
eliminate the casserole and serve the pie from the pan.

1 pound turnips, peeled and cut into cubes
3 cups water
1 pound boiling potatoes, peeled and quartered
1½ teaspoons salt
2 tablespoons vegetable oil
1 cup finely chopped onions
1 cup sliced mushrooms
¼ teaspoon freshly ground black pepper
1 teaspoon dried thyme leaves
3 tablespoons all-purpose flour
4 cups diced cooked lamb

Place the turnips in a pot with the water, cover, and cook over medium heat until
almost tender, 15 to 20 minutes. Add the potatoes and 1 teaspoon of the salt, cover,
and cook until the potatoes are tender, about 15 minutes more. Drain the vegetables,
reserving the water, about 1½ cups of liquid. Using ½ cup of this liquid, mash the vegetables together with a potato masher and set them aside.

Preheat the oven to 425°F. To make the filling, heat the oil in a large heavy-
bottomed skillet over medium-high heat. Add the onions and cook until browned,
about 10 minutes. Add the mushrooms and cook, stirring often, until the onions are
tender and the mushrooms have released their juices, 10 minutes more. Sprinkle on the
remaining ½ teaspoon salt, the pepper, thyme, and flour and stir well. Cook the mixture for 3 minutes and add the remaining cup of reserved liquid. Cook for a few minutes until thickened. Stir in the lamb and spoon into a large ovenproof casserole. Top

with the mashed turnip-and-potato mixture and bake until the top is golden brown, about 20 minutes. Cool 5 minutes before serving.

Moussaka

MAKES 6 SERVINGS

When there is leftover lamb from a roast, take a good hint from Greek cooking and make this casserole. Combining eggplant, tomatoes, and lamb, moussaka has as many versions as meat loaf does. It is a great dish to take to a covered-dish supper because it tastes good hot or warm and reheats well.

2 tablespoons olive oil

½ cup chopped onions

1 clove garlic, peeled and minced

One 28-ounce can diced tomatoes

1 tablespoon minced fresh oregano leaves or 1 teaspoon dried

½ teaspoon ground cinnamon

½ teaspoon salt

¼ teaspoon freshly ground black pepper

4 cups coarsely chopped cooked lamb meat

1 large eggplant, peeled and cut into ¼-inch-thick rounds

1 cup crumbled feta cheese

3 large eggs

1 cup plain yogurt

Heat the oil in a large skillet and cook the onions and garlic over medium heat until softened, about 5 minutes. Stir in the tomatoes, oregano, cinnamon, salt, and pepper. Cook the sauce for 20 minutes. Remove from the heat and stir in the lamb.

Preheat the oven to 350°F. Lightly oil or grease a large casserole, place a layer of eggplant slices on the bottom, and sprinkle with the salt and pepper. Spoon half of the sauce over the eggplant and repeat the layering, ending with eggplant slices. Mix the feta, eggs, and yogurt together in a bowl and spoon over the eggplant. Bake until the top is browned and the eggplant is tender, about 1 hour and 10 minutes. Remove from the oven and let sit for 10 minutes before serving.

Mustard-Maple-Glazed Lamb Chops

MAKES 4 SERVINGS

Lamb chops are a treat and I like to pan-grill these for a supper with good friends. Use a ridged cast-iron skillet or a heavy frying pan.

Lamb loves potatoes cooked and mashed with garlic. Serve with sautéed green beans and a bottle of Merlot.

8 loin lamb chops
Salt and freshly ground black pepper to taste
2 tablespoons country-style grainy mustard mixed with 2 tablespoons pure maple syrup

Preheat the oven to 450°F. Place the skillet over medium heat for several minutes until it sizzles when splashed with a drop of water. Pat the chops dry with paper towels, sprinkle them with salt and pepper, and pan-grill for 2 minutes on each side. Remove from the heat and spread the chops with the mustard-maple mixture.

Place the chops in a lightly oiled ovenproof baking dish and for medium rare chops bake for 10 minutes.

COUNTRY TIPS AND TALES

The secret to keeping chops from curling during cooking is to make a notch through the fat along their outside edge. This technique also works well with steaks and cutlets.

French-Canadian Pork Pie

MAKES 6 TO 8 SERVINGS

Many Vermonters have French-Canadian ancestry, and they remember with great nostalgia the pork pies called *tourtières*. Of course, everyone's mother made the only authentic *tourtière*. Some pies contained only pork, while others mixed beef with pork. Some thickened their pies with crushed crackers and grated potatoes, and others, with flour. My mother-in-law makes this tasty version for Christmas Eve Réveillon, the supper held after Midnight Mass.

A bowl of applesauce or chutney complements the pie, but my husband's family confesses to using ketchup!

FOR THE FILLING

1½ pounds lean ground pork

1 cup finely chopped onions

1 teaspoon minced garlic

½ teaspoon dried thyme leaves

¼ teaspoon ground allspice

½ teaspoon salt

¼ teaspoon freshly ground black pepper

¼ cup all-purpose flour

FOR THE BISCUIT DOUGH

1½ cups all-purpose flour

1½ teaspoons baking powder

1 teaspoon salt

¼ cup vegetable shortening

½ cup plus 1 tablespoon milk

Preheat the oven to 425°F. To make the filling, cook the pork with the onions, garlic, thyme, allspice, salt, and pepper in a large skillet over medium heat, stirring occasionally, until the pork loses all pinkness, 5 to 6 minutes. Sprinkle with the flour and cook 3 to 4 minutes longer, stirring the mixture well. Set the meat aside to cool.

continued

To make the crust, place the flour, baking powder, and salt in a small bowl and stir to combine. Cut the shortening into the flour with a pastry blender or rub it in with your fingers until the mixture resembles oatmeal. Stir in the ½ cup milk with a fork just until the dough gathers into a ball. Turn the dough out onto a lightly floured work table and knead 10 to 12 times. Divide the dough in half and roll one half with a floured rolling pin into a 12-inch circle. Fit it into a 9- or 9½-inch pie plate and spoon in the filling. Lightly flour the surface and roll out the remaining dough into a 12-inch circle and drape it over the filling. Trim off the excess dough and crimp the edges with a fork to seal. Cut several steam vents in the top crust, and brush it with the remaining tablespoon milk. Bake until the pie is golden brown, 20 to 30 minutes. Let rest for 10 minutes before slicing.

Cider Jelly–Basted Pork Roast

MAKES 6 TO 8 SERVINGS

Fair Haven's Methodist church raises much of its winter-fuel money by holding monthly roast pork suppers. The congregation limits the tickets to one hundred people each month and so it knows exactly how much food to cook. Second helpings are encouraged.

Willis and Tina Wood and their family have been making cider jelly in Springfield, Vermont, since the 1880s (see Mail-Order Sources, page 255). The tart and sweet jelly is a counterpoint to the rich flavor of the pork.

One 3-pound boneless pork loin
Salt and freshly ground black pepper to taste
1 cup cider jelly
2 cups water
2 tablespoons cornstarch
½ cup heavy cream

Preheat the oven to 350°F. Generously salt and pepper the meat on all sides and place it fat side up on a rack in a roasting pan. Melt the cider jelly in a small saucepan over low heat and brush some over the meat. Roast the pork, basting every 20 minutes with the jelly. Add 1 cup of the water to the roasting pan after 1 hour. When an instant meat thermometer inserted into the thickest part of the roast reads 150°F, remove the meat to rest for 15 minutes. One-quarter cup of the jelly should remain in the saucepan.

To make a pan gravy from the drippings, skim all the fat from the liquid. Add the remaining cup of water and scrape up all the browned bits from the pan. Pour this back into the saucepan containing the remaining melted cider jelly and bring it to a boil. In a small bowl, stir the cornstarch and cream together until smooth, then whisk into the boiling liquid; it will thicken quickly. Reduce the heat to medium-low and cook the gravy while you cut the meat. Pour any accumulated juices from the cutting board into the gravy and adjust the seasoning. Spoon some gravy over the sliced meat and pass the remainder.

COUNTRY TIPS AND TALES

ROAST PORK FAIR HAVEN METHODIST CHURCH
Mashed spuds, Gravy, Salad, Vegetables,
Pie for Dessert, Beverages
Saturday, November 19 5 to 7 P.M.
Adults $7.50-Children $3.00
ALL ARE WELCOME

Apple-and-Onion-Stuffed Pork Chops

Too often pork chops are overcooked, leaving them dry and tough. This stuffing keeps the meat moist while adding to the flavor. Braised red cabbage and Little Maple-Glazed Squashes (see page 147) would make good accompaniments to this savory supper dish.

- 2 tablespoons unsalted butter
- 1 cup chopped onions
- 2 tart cooking apples, such as greening or Granny Smith, cored, peeled, and coarsely chopped
- ½ teaspoon dried thyme leaves
- ½ teaspoon salt, plus more for sprinkling
- ¼ teaspoon freshly ground black pepper, plus more for sprinkling
- ½ cup fresh whole-wheat bread crumbs
- 4 thick-cut rib or loin pork chops
- 2 teaspoons vegetable oil

Heat the butter in a large skillet over medium heat and cook the onions, stirring occasionally, until softened, about 5 minutes. Stir in the apples, thyme, salt, and pepper and cook for 5 minutes. Remove from the heat and stir in the bread crumbs. Let the mixture cool.

With a sharp knife, cut a pocket into each chop from the fat edge almost to the bone. Stuff the chops with the apple-onion stuffing, then sprinkle them with salt and pepper.

Heat the oil in a large skillet over medium-high heat and cook the chops until no pink shows near the bone, about 5 minutes on each side. Turn them carefully.

Harvest Squash and Pork Stew

MAKES 4 TO 6 SERVINGS

Inspired by the crop of butternut squash that sprang from our compost pile, this cumin-scented stew uses the squash in a piquant manner. This is good with hot steamed rice.

1 tablespoon vegetable oil

2 pounds country-style pork ribs, all visible fat removed and
    cut into 1-inch cubes

1 cup chopped onions

2 cloves garlic, peeled and minced

½ teaspoon crushed cumin seeds

1 to 2 fresh jalapeño chiles, seeded and chopped, or to taste

2 cups peeled and chopped ripe tomatoes or canned diced tomatoes

1 cinnamon stick

1 teaspoon salt

¼ teaspoon freshly ground black pepper

2 cups 1-inch cubes peeled butternut squash

1 cup cooked fresh corn kernels or thawed frozen corn

Heat the oil in a large skillet over high heat and add the meat, onions, garlic, cumin, and chiles. Cook, stirring often, until the meat starts to color and the onions are softened, about 10 minutes. Stir in the tomatoes, cinnamon stick, salt, and pepper, bring to a boil, cover, reduce the heat to medium-low, and cook for 1 hour. Add the squash and corn and cook until the meat and squash are tender, about 20 minutes. Skim the fat from the sauce and adjust the seasoning.

COUNTRY TIPS AND TALES

Loretta Fuller, aged 88, wrote in her diary, "I'm as good as any man. Married 18 years. Husband sick one half the time. Did all the work and had three boarders. I done chores and cut up 2 hogs in one day."
—*Green Mountain Whittlin's*

My Favorite Meat Loaf

MAKES 6 TO 8 SERVINGS

Phooey on those who look down their noses at meat loaf, but simper snidely when eating pâté. Why, pâté is nothing more than a fatty meat loaf! A well-made, juicy meat loaf makes a great supper and nothing beats a cold meat-loaf sandwich the next day.

1 pound bulk Italian sausage

1 pound lean ground beef

2 large eggs

1 cup finely chopped onions

1 cup dried bread crumbs

1 teaspoon dried basil

1 teaspoon dried marjoram

1 teaspoon salt

¼ teaspoon freshly ground black pepper

2 cups bottled chili sauce or barbecue sauce

Preheat the oven to 400°F. Place all the ingredients except the chili sauce in a large bowl and mix well with your hands. Mix in 1 cup of the chili sauce. Scrape the meat mixture into a baking dish and form it into a loaf. Pour the remaining chili sauce on top of the meat loaf. Bake until the loaf is firm to the touch and well browned, about 1 hour. Pour off any accumulated fat from the pan. Let the meat loaf rest 10 minutes before slicing.

Polish Cabbage and Sausage

MAKES 4 TO 6 SERVINGS

Although the Polish school has long closed, West Rutland's Saint Stanislaw Kosta Church still celebrates mass in Polish.

Garlicky kielbasa can be found fresh at Easter and the stuffed dumplings called pierogis are big sellers at the local supermarket. At a recent tasting supper, there were many versions of stuffed cabbage to be sampled.

An old children's taunt, "Oh, go on, you've got eyes like a potato and ears like a cabbage," doesn't stop us from enjoying this dish on a cold winter evening.

1 pound kielbasa, cut into ½-inch-thick slices

1 cup slivered onions

8 cups coarsely shredded green cabbage

1 teaspoon crushed caraway seeds

½ teaspoon brown sugar

½ teaspoon salt

¼ teaspoon freshly ground black pepper

1 tablespoon chopped fresh dill

Place the kielbasa in a large skillet and cook over medium heat until it renders some fat and begins to brown, about 5 minutes. Add the onions, cabbage, and caraway seeds and toss the mixture together. Sprinkle with the sugar, salt, and pepper and cover the pan. Reduce the heat to medium-low and cook, stirring occasionally, until the cabbage is tender, about 30 minutes. Spoon into a serving dish and sprinkle with the dill.

Town Meeting Beans and Bacon

The first Tuesday in March is Town Meeting day. Residents in every town in Vermont still meet to discuss and vote upon local budgets and other state concerns. Elsie Masterton described in *Nothing Whatever to Do* how she and her husband, John, arrived at their first community supper in Goshen. They brought their contribution to the potluck table, but when it came time to eat, no one had told them they needed to bring plates and silverware as well. John had to drive home and fetch the tableware so that they could eat.

The Pumpkin Date Loaf (page 212) or Brown-Bread Muffins (page 128) make good partners for any bean supper. You can also bake the beans in a bean pot or casserole in the oven at 325°F for 4 to 5 hours, but I can't honestly taste the difference!

2 cups dried beans, such as Soldier, Great Northern, or Yellow Eye, soaked
    overnight in water to cover or use the quick-soak method (page 3)

4 thick slices country-smoked bacon

½ cup slivered onions

¼ cup pure dark amber or grade B maple syrup

2 tablespoons prepared mustard

½ teaspoon freshly ground black pepper

1 bay leaf

1 teaspoon dried thyme leaves

1 teaspoon salt

Drain the beans from their soaking water. Cook the bacon over medium heat in a large skillet until most of the fat is rendered but the bacon is not crisp. Drain the strips on paper towels and coarsely chop them.

Place the bacon, onions, beans, maple syrup, mustard, pepper, bay leaf, and thyme in a Dutch oven. Add cold water to cover and bring to a boil over medium heat. Reduce the heat to medium-low and cook, partially covered, for 40 minutes. Uncover and cook until the liquid is almost absorbed by the beans and the beans are tender, about 40 minutes more. Stir in the salt (if you stir it in earlier in the cooking process, the beans will toughen).

Baked Ham with Fall Vegetables

People line up hours ahead to get into the Shrewsbury Fire Department's renowned Ham Supper. Not only is the food delicious, but also the supper is held in the town hall, a beautifully classic New England Congregational Church, at the peak of the fall foliage.

Thelma Perry, who has been cooking for the Rotary Club in nearby Wallingford for forty-odd years, tells me that it is hard to go wrong when cooking a Wallingford Locker ham. One of the last of the local smokehouses/butcher shops, the locker sells the best ham, sweet and smoky. Don't forget to save the bone for making soup.

One 6- to 7-pound smoked ham, trimmed of excess fat
Freshly ground black pepper to taste
4 large carrots, cut into thin strips
1 large celery root, peeled and cut into thin strips
1 medium-size rutabaga, peeled and cut into thin strips
4 large parsnips, peeled, cored, and cut into thin strips
2 cups apple cider
Salt to taste

Preheat the oven to 325°F. Place the ham fat side up in a roasting pan and sprinkle generously with pepper. Roast for 1 hour, then add the vegetables and cider, cover, and cook until an instant meat thermometer inserted into the thickest part of the meat reads 160°F, about 1 hour more.

Remove the ham to a platter to rest and cover it loosely with a sheet of aluminum foil to keep warm. Tilt the roasting pan to skim off any fat. Season the vegetables with salt and pepper and spoon them into a heated serving bowl. Slice the ham at the table.

Baked Fresh Ham with Garlic

MAKES 10 TO 12 SERVINGS

Many families serve a fresh ham instead of smoked ham at holiday time. The aroma while roasting lures folks to the kitchen. Good partners to this roast are Rutabaga Gratin (page 145) and mashed potatoes.

One 10-pound fresh ham, shank portion, skin removed and trimmed of
    excess fat
6 large cloves garlic, peeled
2 bay leaves
1 teaspoon fennel seeds
1 teaspoon dried rosemary
1 teaspoon dried marjoram
1 tablespoon black peppercorns
1 tablespoon kosher salt

Place the ham in a roasting pan that will fit in the refrigerator. Put the garlic, herbs, and pepper and salt in a mortar and pound them into a paste or use a blender or a mini food processor. Rub this paste over the ham. Cover it with plastic wrap and refrigerate overnight. Remove the ham from the refrigerator 1 hour before baking to allow it to come to room temperature.

Preheat the oven to 350°F. Bake the ham, uncovered, until an instant meat thermometer inserted into the thickest part of the meat reads 150°F, about 3 hours. Remove from the oven and let the meat rest for 15 minutes before slicing. Cover it loosely with a sheet of aluminum foil to keep warm.

Poultry and Game
Supper Dishes

CHICKEN AND BISCUITS, CHICKEN pie, and chicken barbecue are among the most common community suppers offered. Now our favorite bird, chicken was once a great luxury and not common table fare. Eggs were the more coveted product and only the old layers were stewed. My husband grew up on a poultry farm and is insistent on quality chicken. If there isn't a source of organic chickens available, I urge you to search out the least processed, whitest, freshest bird you can find.

Chicken lends itself to the gamut of preparations, from a simple roast to a fancy sauté. When teaching a class on chicken know-how, I like to show my students how to get many meals from one bird. I tell them to cut the breasts into strips for a stir-fry, cook the legs and thighs in a fricassee, make soup from the carcass and giblets, and make a bonus treat for the cook by sautéing the liver with some onions to make a spread for rye bread. That's smart cooking!

Vermonters raise many turkeys, especially for the holiday season. It is a very popular bird to serve at community suppers, either as a roast or in a pie. Many people like only the white meat, but at our house everyone prefers the dark. Luckily, turkey parts have become easy to find and use all year-round, satisfying everyone's tastes. If you go to a turkey social, expect not only to eat turkey, but also to play cards, gamble a little, and have a good time.

Once a common supper dish, rabbit is rarely seen on home tables, although still served regularly in Europe and found in gourmet restaurants here. It seems a shame not to bring rabbit back into our repertoire of dishes. Happily, I have a source of locally raised rabbit. Keeping several in my freezer lets me use this delicious meat in my favorite recipes, which I serve to good friends throughout the year. I encourage you to find a source of rabbit and try these dishes.

Hunting is still a big part of country living and I know several people who take vacations late in the fall just to go deer hunting. Happy are those who go into winter with a freezer full of venison. My neighbors have shared with me their bounty as well as their recipes for preparing venison. Wild turkeys are also seen in the fields gleaning the leftover corn, but I haven't tasted one yet. Perhaps at this year's game suppers, I'll get a chance.

COUNTRY TIPS AND TALES

25TH BENEFIT GAME SUPPER
Tinmouth Volunteer Fire Department
Tinmouth, Vermont
On Saturday, November 19, 1994, the Tinmouth Volunteer
Fire Department will hold its annual GAME SUPPER.
It will take place in the Tinmouth Fire House, just off
Rte. 140. As in the past, the event will start at 5 P.M.
and continue until the food is gone.
This year the menu will include Venison in various forms
such as Roast and Meatloaf, Roasted Coon, Pheasant Pie,
Chicken Pie (for those who do not eat game), Moose, Bear,
and other types of game.
Also on the menu will be various types of salad,
the Famous Tinmouth Pies, Coffee, Tea, and Milk.
Donation: Adults $9.50; Children $4.50; Under 6 yrs. FREE

Chicken Pot Pie

MAKES 6 TO 8 SERVINGS

Topped with a buttery biscuit crust, this supper classic is a family favorite. Loaded with vegetables that can vary with the seasons, tender biscuit-crusted pies like these were staples on country tables. This pie crosses the line into the realm of casseroles and shows up as the star of many church suppers and in a supporting role at potlucks.

FOR THE FILLING

2 tablespoons unsalted butter

1 cup chopped onions

2 large carrots, cut into ½-inch-thick slices

2 stalks celery, cut into ½-inch-thick slices

1 cup sliced mushrooms

3 tablespoons all-purpose flour

1 teaspoon salt (if using canned broth, taste before adding)

¼ teaspoon freshly ground black pepper

3 cups chicken stock (page 2)

½ teaspoon dried thyme or savory leaves

4 cups diced cooked chicken

One 10-ounce package frozen baby peas, thawed

FOR THE BISCUIT CRUST

2 cups all-purpose flour

2 teaspoons baking powder

1 teaspoon baking soda

1 teaspoon sugar

½ teaspoon salt

3 tablespoons cold unsalted butter, cut into pieces

3 tablespoons cold vegetable shortening

1 cup buttermilk

To make the filling, heat the butter in a large skillet over medium heat and cook the onions, carrots, and celery until they begin to soften, about 10 minutes. Add the mushrooms, stir, and cook until the mushrooms soften, about 5 minutes. Sprinkle on the flour, salt, and pepper and stir to mix thoroughly. Cook for 3 minutes, then add the chicken stock and thyme. Bring to a boil and cook until thickened, several minutes longer. Stir in the chicken and peas. Scrape into a shallow 9 × 13-inch baking dish and set aside.

Preheat the oven to 400°F.

To make the crust, stir together the flour, baking powder and soda, sugar, and salt in a medium-size bowl and cut in the butter and shortening with a pastry blender or rub it in with your fingers until the mixture resembles oatmeal. Stir in the buttermilk with a fork to form a soft dough. Place rounded tablespoonfuls of the dough over the chicken filling, leaving space between each spoonful. Bake until the top is golden brown and the filling is bubbling, 30 to 40 minutes.

COUNTRY TIPS AND TALES

If you need to make pot pies for a crowd, they will bake better if made in several shallow pans rather than in one deep pan.

Chicken and Apples in Cream

MAKES 4 TO 6 SERVINGS

This delicious country dish is similar to those found in the Normandy region of France. Vermont, too, has a bounty of apples and sweet cream and all good country cooks use the foods they have on hand. Serve with Country-Style Greens (page 133) and wild rice for a supper with dear friends.

2 tablespoons unsalted butter

1 large leek, white and tender green parts, thoroughly washed
   and finely chopped

2 tart apples, such as greening or Granny Smith, cored, peeled,
   and thinly sliced

2 tablespoons all-purpose flour

1 teaspoon salt

¼ teaspoon freshly ground black pepper

1 cup chicken stock

½ cup heavy cream

Few drops of fresh lemon juice

4 cups shredded cooked chicken

1 tablespoon finely chopped fresh chives

Heat the butter in a large skillet over medium heat and cook the leeks, stirring, until softened and beginning to brown, about 10 minutes. Add the apples and cook, stirring occasionally, until softened, about 10 minutes. Sprinkle on the flour, salt, and pepper and stir. Cook 3 minutes, then add the stock and cream. Cook 3 to 5 minutes, until the sauce is thickened. Season with the lemon juice, stir in the chicken, and heat through. Sprinkle with the chives and serve.

COUNTRY TIPS AND TALES

Poaching chicken for use in many dishes is simple and yields meat that is juicy and tender. I learned this useful technique in a Chinese cooking class and happily pass it on to you. Heat 3 quarts of water to boiling, put in a whole chicken (up to 4 pounds), bring the water back to a boil, cover, turn off the heat, and let it stand for 1 hour. Then remove the chicken, remove the skin, and take the meat off the bones. Return the bones and skin to the liquid and cook 1 hour to make a light chicken stock. One 3½-pound chicken will yield 4 cups of cooked chicken chunks.

Stewed Chicken with Herbed Dumplings

MAKES 6 TO 8 SERVINGS

Old hens were cooked up slowly in a soup kettle for hours to make them tender; the dumplings were added just before serving. My late friend Mary Reed, a Vermont native who cooked in lumber camps and raised horses, always welcomed visitors with a pot of chicken and dumplings.

Finding soup chickens is pretty difficult these days, rare commodity that they are, and so we must make do with a broiler-fryer. These chickens no longer have to simmer for 3 hours to become tender.

FOR THE CHICKEN STEW

One 3½-pound chicken

1 cup slivered onions

3 carrots, cut into 2-inch chunks

4 stalks celery, cut into 2-inch chunks

1 bay leaf

1 teaspoon dried thyme leaves

2 teaspoons salt

½ teaspoon freshly ground black pepper

FOR THE HERB DUMPLINGS

2 cups all-purpose flour

4 teaspoons baking powder

¼ teaspoon salt

¼ teaspoon freshly ground black pepper

1 tablespoon snipped fresh chives

1 tablespoon finely chopped fresh parsley leaves

1 tablespoon cold unsalted butter, cut into pieces

2 tablespoons cold vegetable shortening

¾ cup milk

To make the stew, place the chicken in a 5-quart soup pot and cover with cold water. Bring to a boil over medium-high heat and skim off any foam. Add the vegetables, bay leaf, thyme, salt, and pepper, reduce the heat to medium-low, and cook until the chicken is very tender, about 1½ hours. Carefully remove the chicken to a platter and let it cool. Remove the bones and skin. Cut the meat into 1-inch cubes. Skim off any fat and measure 6 cups of broth (freeze any extra for another use). Adjust the seasonings. Return the chicken to the pot and continue to cook over medium-low heat.

To make dumplings, place the flour, baking powder, salt, pepper, and herbs in a medium-size bowl and stir together. Cut in the butter and shortening with a pastry blender or rub it in with your fingers until the mixture resembles oatmeal. Stir in the milk with a fork to form a soft dough. Drop rounded tablespoonfuls of dough onto the chicken, cover tightly, and cook until the tops of the dumplings look dry, 15 to 20 minutes. Serve in shallow soup plates.

COUNTRY TIPS AND TALES

It's bad luck to those who give a chicken away.
Something must be given or paid for it.
—Ferne Sheton, *Pioneer Superstitions*

Macaroni and Chicken in Cheddar Sauce

MAKES 4 TO 6 SERVINGS

At potluck suppers this tasty version of macaroni and cheese disappears first, proving that even mundane meals can have new life. This is an easily made casserole when you have leftovers from a roasted or poached chicken. Use an extra-sharp Cheddar for the best flavor.

2 cups elbow macaroni

¼ cup (½ stick) unsalted butter

¼ cup all-purpose flour

2 cups chicken stock (page 2)

2 cups milk

2 cups shredded extra-sharp Cheddar cheese

1 teaspoon salt (if using canned broth, taste before adding)

¼ teaspoon freshly ground black pepper

Few pinches of cayenne pepper

2 cups 1-inch cubes cooked chicken

1 cup dried bread crumbs

Cook the macaroni in a large pot of salted boiling water for 4 minutes. Drain and rinse in cold water until cool and drain again.

Preheat the oven to 425°F. Heat the butter in a medium-size saucepan over medium heat. When it is bubbling, whisk in the flour and cook, stirring, for 2 minutes. Add the stock and milk and heat until boiling, stirring constantly. Let the sauce boil for 1 minute, then remove from the heat. Add 1 cup of the Cheddar, the salt, pepper, and cayenne and stir until smooth. Fold in the chicken. Drain the macaroni completely and fold it into the sauce. Scoop into a shallow medium-size baking dish. Toss the remaining cup of Cheddar together with the bread crumbs and sprinkle evenly over the top. Bake until the top is browned and the contents are bubbling, 20 to 30 minutes.

COUNTRY TIPS AND TALES

Wing's Cheese Store, in Thetford, advertised in 1963 in *Rural Vermonter:* "Truly-aged cheddar; Waxed Wheels, real SAGE cheese; Rat-Trap-King of the Cheeses, since 1928."

Sunday Roast Chicken

MAKES 6 TO 8 SERVINGS

Gourmet chefs are rediscovering it; cookbook writers write treatises about it; and folks are just plain nostalgic at the thought of it. A juicy, plump, crisp-skinned bird, big enough for supper and lots of chicken sandwiches served on Buttermilk Bread (page 116) later on in the week. Serve with Garden Colcannon (page 143) and Dilled Peas and Mushrooms (page 148) for a Sunday supper with good company.

> One 6- to 8-pound roasting chicken
> 1 lemon
> Salt and freshly ground black pepper to taste
>
> FOR OPTIONAL GRAVY
> 2 cups chicken stock (page 2)
> 2 tablespoons cornstarch
> ⅓ cup heavy cream
> Salt and freshly ground black pepper to taste

Preheat the oven to 425°F. Wash and dry the chicken inside and out and remove the excess fat from the neck and cavity. (Freeze the giblets and liver for another use.) Cut the lemon in half and rub one half over the skin of the chicken and place the other half in the bird. Salt and pepper the chicken inside and out. Place the chicken, breast up, on a rack in a roasting pan and roast for 30 minutes. Reduce the heat to 350°F. Baste the chicken with the pan drippings every 20 minutes until the internal temperature reads 170°F when an instant meat thermometer is inserted into the thigh of the chicken, about 1 hour. Remove the chicken to a platter and cover loosely with a sheet of aluminum foil to keep it warm. Let rest 15 minutes before carving.

To make gravy, skim off the fat from the roasting pan. Add the chicken stock and scrape up all the browned bits. Pour into a saucepan and bring to a boil over medium heat. In a small bowl, whisk the cornstarch with the heavy cream until smooth and stir into the boiling liquid. Let boil a minute, reduce the heat to medium-low, and cook for 5 minutes. Add any accumulated juices from the chicken and season the gravy with salt and pepper.

Jerk Chicken

How small the world has become! Every autumn a group of men from Jamaica, West Indies, arrive in Shoreham, high above Lake Champlain, to harvest apples. They have joined in many a local potluck supper and shared this deliciously spicy example of island cooking. Jerk seasoning is available in the condiment section at the supermarket. My favorite is Walkerwood or Busha Brown's—very aromatic and very hot! So resist the temptation to add even a little more.

One 3½-pound chicken
1 to 2 tablespoons jerk seasoning

Remove the backbone from the chicken. Using a very sharp knife, cut down and through the thigh joint on one side of the backbone, continue down along the ribs, staying close to the backbone, and out through the wing joint. Repeat on the other side and spread the chicken flat in a roasting pan. (Save the backbone in the freezer to make soup.) Rub the chicken all over with the jerk seasoning. Cover the chicken with plastic wrap and refrigerate overnight. Remove the chicken from the refrigerator 1 hour before cooking to allow it to come to room temperature.

Preheat the oven to 350°F. Remove the plastic wrap and bake the chicken until the juices run clear when you prick the thighs with a fork, about 1 hour. Cut the chicken into serving pieces and pass the beer.

Chicken Fricassee

There are many versions of fricassee, from plain to fancy, enriched with yolks and cream. My mother remembers her mother cooking chicken with onions, celery, and paprika, but she did not use cream because they kept kosher. Her fricassee is halfway between a sauté and a braise. Serve this with noodles or spätzle.

2 tablespoons vegetable oil

One 3½-pound chicken, cut into 8 pieces, skin left on

1 cup chopped onions

½ cup chopped celery

1 clove garlic, peeled and minced

2 tablespoons all-purpose flour

1 teaspoon sweet Hungarian paprika

1 teaspoon salt (if using canned broth, taste before adding)

¼ teaspoon freshly ground black pepper

1 cup chicken stock (page 2)

1 tablespoon finely chopped fresh parsley leaves

Heat the oil in a large heavy-bottomed skillet over medium heat. Wipe the chicken pieces dry with paper towels and brown well on all sides, 10 to 15 minutes. Remove the chicken from the pan, set aside, and cover loosely with a sheet of aluminum foil to keep warm.

Discard all but 1 tablespoon of the fat in the skillet. Add the onions, celery, and garlic and cook, stirring occasionally, until they start to brown, 12 to 15 minutes. Sprinkle on the flour, paprika, salt, and pepper and cook, stirring, for 2 minutes. Add the stock and cook for 3 minutes, scraping up all the browned bits from the skillet. Return the chicken pieces and any accumulated juices to the skillet. Cover the skillet, reduce the heat to medium-low, and cook until the chicken is tender when pierced with a fork, about 30 minutes. Tilt the pan and skim off the fat. Place the chicken and sauce on a platter and sprinkle with the parsley.

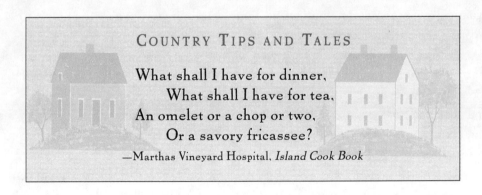

COUNTRY TIPS AND TALES

What shall I have for dinner,
What shall I have for tea,
An omelet or a chop or two,
Or a savory fricassee?
—Marthas Vineyard Hospital, *Island Cook Book*

Dandelion~Stuffed Chicken Breasts

Pick dandelions when they are small, about 4 inches long, and before they have flowered, otherwise they'll be tough and bitter. Of course, pick them only from an unsprayed lawn, one without resident cats or dogs! The supermarket sometimes sells long dandelions that are commercially raised.

Rural Vermonter, in the Fall 1963 issue, tells of one woman's remembrance: "Mother salted dandelions, layered in a crock, pressed down and weighted with a well-scrubbed rock. Months later, they could be freshened in cold water and cooked exactly as if taken from the ground."

> 8 ounces dandelions, stems removed
> 4 strips bacon
> 2 cloves garlic, peeled and minced
> Salt and freshly ground black pepper to taste
> Eight 6-ounce skinless, boneless chicken breast halves
> Flour for dredging
> 2 tablespoons pure olive oil

Wash the dandelions very well in several changes of water. Blanch them for 2 minutes in a large pot of boiling salted water. Drain, refresh with cold water, and drain again. Squeeze the water from the dandelions by rolling them in a clean kitchen towel. Coarsely chop the leaves.

Cut the bacon crosswise into ¼-inch-wide strips and cook, stirring, in a large skillet over medium heat until just crisp, 5 to 7 minutes. Remove the bacon with a slotted spoon to a paper towel to drain. Discard all but 1 tablespoon of the fat from the pan and cook the garlic for 1 minute. Add the dandelions, sprinkle with salt and pepper, and cook, stirring, until tender, about 4 minutes. Remove from the heat, stir in the reserved bacon, and let cool.

Remove the tenderloins from the underside of each breast. Flatten them gently between sheets of waxed paper with your fingers. Make a pocket lengthwise in the breasts. Push the stuffing into the pockets and use the flattened pieces to cover the stuffing completely.

Place the flour on a sheet of waxed paper. Heat the oil in a large skillet over medium heat. Sprinkle the stuffed breasts with salt and pepper and dredge them in flour, coating both sides evenly and shaking off the excess. Cook the breasts in the hot oil until golden brown, 4 to 5 minutes on each side. It is better to cook only four breasts at a time to avoid overcrowding the skillet. Loosely cover the cooked breasts with a sheet of aluminum foil to keep them warm while cooking the remaining breasts.

Crispy Oven-Fried Chicken Breasts

MAKES 6 TO 8 SERVINGS

Cooking chicken breasts by this method keeps them juicy and makes a delicious supper paired with Red and Green Cabbage Salad (page 140). Any leftovers make great sandwiches spread with Cranberry Apple Chutney (page 151) on pumpernickel bread.

2 large eggs

1 tablespoon pure olive oil

½ cup freshly grated Parmesan cheese

1½ cups dried bread crumbs

½ teaspoon salt

¼ teaspoon freshly ground black pepper

Eight 6-ounce skinless, boneless chicken breast halves

Preheat the oven to 450°F. In a shallow bowl, beat the eggs together with a fork. Spread the oil on a baking sheet. Mix the cheese, bread crumbs, salt, and pepper together in a pie plate. Dip each chicken breast in the eggs, then in the crumb mixture to coat completely, and place them on the baking sheet. Bake until golden brown and firm to the touch, about 15 minutes.

Parking Lot Chicken Barbecue

Not every Vermont town is graced with a classic town green, so it is no surprise to see our local fire department grilling chickens in the supermarket parking lot. For this barbecue you will also need corn on the cob, coleslaw, napkins, and a place in the shade to sit and eat.

Two 3½-pound chickens
1 cup cider vinegar
1 tablespoon salt
1 teaspoon freshly ground black pepper

Remove the backbone from the chickens. Using a very sharp knife, cut down and through the thigh joint on one side of the backbone, continue down along the ribs, staying close to the backbone, and cut through the wing joint. Repeat on the other side and spread the chickens flat in a nonreactive pan or platter. (Save the backbone in the freezer to make soup.) Mix the vinegar with the salt and pepper until the salt is dissolved and rub it well into both sides of the chickens. Cover with plastic wrap and refrigerate overnight. Bring to room temperature before cooking.

Preheat the oven to 400°F and prepare the grill. (If you're using charcoal or wood, you'll need a hot bed of coals.) Place the chickens skin up on a baking sheet and roast for 40 minutes, then carefully place them skin down on the grill. Cook for 10 minutes, then turn the chickens over and cook for 10 minutes more. Remove from the fire and let rest 5 minutes before cutting into serving pieces.

COUNTRY TIPS AND TALES

Somehow, when grilling chicken at home, you always end up with raw insides and burned skin. For that reason, I often cheat and precook the chicken in the oven, then throw it on the grill for a short time to get the flavor.

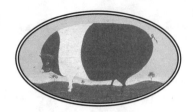

Roast Turkey with Sausage Stuffing

MAKES 12 TO 16 SERVINGS

I like to cook small turkeys between 12 and 16 pounds. This is bucking the trend of bigger is better. Not only do you save your back from lifting a humongous 25-pound bird, but small turkeys cook more quickly and evenly. At Spring Lake Ranch, where we raised turkeys, I roasted 10 birds for last Thanksgiving's meal.

For those who love only the white meat, see the recipe for Apple and Walnut–Stuffed Turkey Breast on page 60. I prefer a more reasonable proportion of dark meat to white because I love dark meat. Make the stock and stuffing the day before to save some time.

One 12- to 16-pound turkey

1 medium-size onion, unpeeled, cut into quarters

1 stalk celery, quartered

8 cups cold water

FOR THE STUFFING

1 pound breakfast sausage meat

1 cup finely chopped onions

1 cup finely chopped celery

8 cups whole-wheat bread cubes

2 tablespoons minced fresh parsley leaves

1 teaspoon dried thyme leaves

½ teaspoon crumbled dried sage leaves

2 teaspoons salt

1 teaspoon freshly ground black pepper

2 large eggs, lightly beaten

FOR BASTING

2 tablespoons unsalted butter

2 tablespoons vegetable oil

FOR THE GRAVY

¼ cup all-purpose flour

Salt and freshly ground pepper to taste

To prepare the turkey, remove the giblets and neck from the turkey, place them with the quartered onion and celery in a 3-quart saucepan, and cover with the water. Cut off the wing tips from the turkey and add them to the pot. Bring to a boil over medium heat, reduce the heat to medium-low, and cook, partially covered, for 1½ hours. Strain the stock through a fine-meshed sieve. If you wish, pick the meat off the neck bone and chop it with the giblets. Reserve this meat, refrigerated, for the gravy. You will need 5 cups of turkey stock for the stuffing and gravy.

To make the stuffing, crumble the sausage into a large skillet over medium heat and cook until the fat is rendered and the meat browned, 5 to 7 minutes. Stir in the chopped onions and celery and cook until the vegetable are softened, about 5 minutes. Scrape into a large bowl and mix in the bread, parsley, thyme, sage, 1 teaspoon of the salt, and ½ teaspoon of the pepper. Stir the mixture together, adding 1 cup of the stock and the eggs. Mix the stuffing well; it should be thoroughly moistened. Add a bit more stock if necessary.

Preheat the oven to 425°F. Rinse the turkey inside and out and pat dry. Remove excess fat from the neck and cavity. Season the turkey inside and out with the remaining teaspoon salt and ½ teaspoon pepper and loosely stuff the body cavity and the neck cavity, if there is enough stuffing. Tie the legs together with kitchen twine. Skewer the skin to keep the neck cavity closed. Place the turkey, breast up, on a rack in a roasting pan. Heat the butter with the oil and brush on the turkey. Cook for 30 minutes, reduce the oven temperature to 350°F, and continue to cook for 2½ to 3 hours longer, basting with the butter-oil mixture and the pan drippings every 30 minutes. If the skin is browning too much, loosely cover the turkey with aluminum foil.

Test the turkey by inserting an instant meat thermometer into the thickest part of the thigh. It should read 180°F. The thigh joints will move easily and the juices run clear. Remove the turkey to a platter and cover loosely with a sheet of foil to keep it warm. Let it rest for 30 minutes before slicing.

continued

To make the gravy, place 4 cups of the reserved stock in a saucepan and bring to a boil over medium heat. Make a pan gravy by removing all but ¼ cup of the fat from the roasting pan. Place the pan over medium heat and whisk in the flour, scraping up the browned bits, and stir for several minutes. Pour in the boiling stock and let cook until the gravy thickens. Add any accumulated juices from the turkey platter, add the reserved chopped meat, and adjust the seasoning. Pour into a warmed gravy boat.

Remove any skewers and string from the turkey and spoon out the stuffing into a serving bowl. Carve the turkey and pass the Cranberry Apple Chutney (page 151).

COUNTRY TIPS AND TALES

Remember, once you have stuffed the turkey, roast it immediately to prevent any bacteria from growing.

Apple and Walnut–Stuffed Turkey Breast

MAKES 10 TO 12 SERVINGS

So many people prefer white meat only that turkey growers are selling more breasts than whole turkeys. This recipe is delicious hot or cold and lends itself perfectly to a buffet supper table. If you can only find three-pound boneless breasts, buy two and divide the stuffing between them. They will take less time to roast, so check the temperature after an hour.

¼ cup unsalted butter

1 cup chopped onions

1 cup diced celery

4 apples, cored, peeled, and diced

1 teaspoon salt, plus more for sprinkling

½ teaspoon crumbled dried sage

½ teaspoon freshly ground black pepper, plus more for sprinkling

2 cups whole-wheat bread cubes

2 large eggs, lightly beaten

1 cup turkey or chicken stock (page 2)

One 6-pound boneless turkey breast, thawed if frozen

Heat 2 tablespoons of the butter in a large skillet over medium heat and add the onions, celery, and apples. Cook, stirring until softened and beginning to brown, 7 to 9 minutes. Remove from the stove and let cool. Stir in ½ teaspoon of the salt, the sage, ¼ teaspoon of the pepper, the bread cubes, eggs, and stock. Mix well.

Preheat the oven to 325°F. Grease a 9 × 13-inch baking pan. Open the turkey breast and place it skin side down. Remove the small tenderloin from each side of the breast and remove the white tendons with a sharp knife. Place the tenderloins on each side of the breast. Sprinkle with salt and pepper and place the stuffing down the center of the breast. Fold the sides over the stuffing to make a neat package and skewer together, securing with kitchen twine. Place seam side down in the baking pan. Sprinkle with the remaining ½ teaspoon salt and ¼ teaspoon pepper and melt the remaining butter in a small saucepan to use for basting. Baste every 20 minutes. Roast, uncovered, until an instant meat thermometer inserted in the thickest part reads 170° to 175°F, about 1¼ hours.

Remove to a serving platter and cover loosely with a sheet of aluminum foil to keep it warm. Let it rest for 15 minutes before slicing.

Creamed Turkey with Cornmeal Biscuits

MAKES 6 TO 8 SERVINGS

At a turkey pie supper in Ascutney, I chatted with an elderly woman and her three daughters who encouraged my husband and me to cross the river to Cornish, New Hampshire, to try another supper. Spanning the broad Connecticut River is a long, covered wooden bridge connecting the two states. We felt as though we were crossing a time line back to the last century as we entered this sleepy hamlet on the river.

FOR THE TURKEY

3 tablespoons unsalted butter

¼ cup all-purpose flour

4 cups hot turkey stock (page 2)

½ cup milk

6 cups 1-inch-cubed cooked turkey meat

Salt and freshly ground black pepper to taste

FOR THE BISCUIT TOPPING

1 cup stone-ground white or yellow cornmeal

1 cup all-purpose flour

1 tablespoon firmly packed light brown sugar

2 teaspoons baking powder

1 teaspoon baking soda

¼ teaspoon salt

3 tablespoons chilled vegetable shortening

2 tablespoons unsalted butter

¾ cup fresh buttermilk

To prepare the turkey, heat the butter in a large skillet over medium heat and stir in the flour. Cook for several minutes, stirring often, then whisk in the stock and milk. Bring to a boil, stirring constantly, until thickened and smooth. Reduce the heat to medium-low and cook the sauce for 3 minutes. Remove from the heat, stir in the turkey, and season with salt and pepper. Pour into a shallow medium-size casserole and set aside.

Preheat the oven to 400°F. Place the cornmeal, flour, sugar, baking powder and soda, and salt in a bowl and stir to combine. Cut the shortening and butter into the flour mixture using a pastry blender or rub it in with your fingers until the mixture resembles oatmeal. Stir in the buttermilk with a fork to make a soft dough. Drop spoonfuls of the dough on the creamed turkey, leaving spaces between each spoonful. Bake until the biscuits are golden brown and the sauce is bubbling, 25 to 30 minutes.

Pan-fried Turkey Cutlets

MAKES 4 TO 6 SERVINGS

A quick supper dish using sliced turkey breast cutlets cooked with a garnish of lemon, garlic, and parsley. Serve with a pilaf of rice and Cider-Glazed Carrots (page 146) for a colorful supper any time of the year.

2 pounds turkey cutlets
½ cup all-purpose flour
3 tablespoons cornmeal
½ teaspoon salt
¼ teaspoon freshly ground black pepper
3 tablespoons pure olive oil
1 tablespoon finely chopped fresh parsley leaves
Grated rind of 1 lemon
1 clove garlic, peeled and minced

Cut the turkey cutlets into strips 1 inch wide by 2 inches long. Place the flour, cornmeal, salt, and pepper in a plastic bag. Heat 2 tablespoons of the oil in a large skillet over high heat. Shake half the turkey strips in the flour mixture, shake off any excess flour, and carefully cook them in the hot oil until they lose all pinkness and begin to brown, 2 to 3 minutes. Set these aside and cover loosely with a sheet of aluminum foil to stay warm while you cook the remaining turkey.

Add the remaining tablespoon oil to the pan and stir in the parsley, lemon rind, and garlic. Cook for 1 minute and return the turkey strips and any accumulated juices to the pan. Toss and reheat briefly.

Turkey Cheddar Burgers

This makes a quick supper served on crusty rolls with a slice of summer-ripe tomato after a long day of gardening or hiking in the Green Mountains. Great Grandma Hoff's Open Crock Pickles (page 154) provide a tangy contrast to the flavor of the turkey.

    2 pounds ground turkey
    3 tablespoons olive oil
    ½ cup finely chopped scallions
    ½ teaspoon salt
    ¼ teaspoon freshly ground black pepper
    6 slices sharp Cheddar cheese

Place the turkey in a mixing bowl. Heat 2 tablespoons of the oil in a small skillet over medium heat and cook the scallions until softened, about 4 minutes. Mix the scallions, salt, and pepper into the turkey. Shape the mixture into 6 patties. Heat the remaining tablespoon oil in a large nonstick skillet over medium heat and cook the patties for 4 minutes. Turn them over and place a slice of Cheddar on each one. Cook until the cheese has melted, another 4 to 5 minutes.

Curry-Braised Turkey

Now that turkey parts are widely available, making this dish is easy. Aromatic curry powder, fresh ginger, and some hot pepper sauce (I use Trappey's) give the dish its piquant flavor, but do adjust the pepper sauce to suit your own taste. Serve over basmati rice.

3½ pounds turkey legs and thighs

1 tablespoon vegetable oil

1 cup slivered onions

1 tablespoon peeled and minced fresh ginger

1 clove garlic, peeled and minced

1 teaspoon curry powder

½ teaspoon salt

¼ teaspoon freshly ground black pepper

1 cup apple cider

2 teaspoons hot pepper sauce

1 tablespoon cornstarch

1 scallion, finely chopped

With a sharp knife, remove the skin from the turkey legs. Remove the meat from the bones and cut into 2-inch pieces. Save the skin and bones in the freezer for future stock making.

Heat the oil in a large skillet over medium heat and cook the onions, ginger, and garlic, stirring occasionally, until softened, about 5 minutes. Sprinkle in the curry powder and cook 2 minutes longer. Add the turkey pieces, salt, and pepper and stir well. Add ½ cup of the apple cider and bring to a boil. Cover, reduce the heat to low, and cook until the turkey is tender, about 30 minutes. Stir together the remaining ½ cup apple cider, the hot sauce, and cornstarch until smooth and stir into the sauce. Bring to a boil and cook until just thickened, about 2 minutes. Spoon into a serving dish and sprinkle with the chopped scallion.

COUNTRY TIPS AND TALES

According to the United States Department of Agriculture, the 1993 yearly consumption of chicken and turkey accounts for 32 percent of the total amount of meat consumed in the United States, up from 17 percent in 1970.

—*The New York Times*, November 13, 1996

Rabbit Sautéed with Wild Leeks

MAKES 4 TO 6 SERVINGS

Wild leeks, or ramps, are a springtime forager's delight. Like fiddlehead ferns, these garlicky leeks seem to be there just to awaken the taste buds after the long winter. Look in the woods, usually under some maples, for spadelike 5- to 7-inch-long deep green leaves with maroon stems above a white bulb. Wash well and discard the leaves, using only the plump white bulb. If you can't get these leeks, substitute shallots and garlic. The dish will still be robustly aromatic. Serve with My Half-Whole-Wheat Loaf (page 113) to mop up the sauce.

3 tablespoons olive oil

2 cups wild leek bulbs, thoroughly washed and root ends trimmed, or

    1 cup shallots, sliced, and 2 cloves garlic, peeled and minced

One 2- to 2½-pound rabbit, skinned and cut into 6 pieces

½ cup all-purpose flour

½ teaspoon salt

¼ teaspoon freshly ground black pepper

⅔ cup water

Heat 1½ tablespoons of the oil in a large, heavy-bottomed skillet over medium heat. Cook the leeks, stirring, until they begin to color, 5 to 7 minutes. Remove the leeks and set aside. Add the remaining 1½ tablespoons oil to the skillet. Dredge the rabbit pieces in the flour, tapping off any excess, and brown them on both sides. Sprinkle with the salt and pepper, and add the reserved leeks and water to the skillet. Cover and cook, turning the pieces once, until the breast and saddle meat are tender when pierced with a fork, about 25 minutes. Remove them to a dish and cover loosely with a sheet of aluminum foil to keep them warm. Cook the legs about 5 minutes longer. Skim any fat from the gravy, return the reserved meat to the skillet, and reheat before serving.

Rabbit Cacciatore

MAKES 4 TO 6 SERVINGS

The South End Market, in Rutland, owned by Sal and Ted Salerni, is one of the last of the neighborhood grocery-butcher stores. It is always a pleasure to chat with these expert meat cutters. Their brother-in-law, Barrie Byrne, has been raising rabbits for fifty years for their market, and has many delicious recipes to share.

Pasta or polenta, a dish of sautéed greens like escarole or broccoli rabe, an Italian wine, and a simple fruit for dessert will make this supper complete.

One 2- to 2½-pound rabbit, skinned and cut into 6 pieces
1 teaspoon salt
Freshly ground black pepper to taste
2 tablespoons pure olive oil
1 cup sliced onions
2 cloves garlic, peeled and minced
2 cups (6 ounces) quartered mushrooms
1 tablespoon fresh rosemary leaves or 1 teaspoon dried
1 cup dry white wine
2 cups canned crushed tomatoes

continued

Sprinkle the rabbit pieces with the salt and pepper. Place the oil in a large skillet over medium-high heat and brown the rabbit on all sides. Stir in the remaining ingredients and bring to a boil. Cover, reduce the heat to medium-low, and cook for 15 minutes. Turn the rabbit pieces over in the sauce. Cover and cook until the rabbit breasts feel tender when pierced with a fork, about 10 minutes more. Remove the breast and saddle meat, cover loosely with a sheet of aluminum foil to keep them warm, and cook the legs another 5 minutes. Return the reserved rabbit pieces to the sauce and skim any fat from the sauce. Adjust the seasonings before serving.

COUNTRY TIPS AND TALES

Rabbit is usually cut into six parts, two leg portions, two saddles, and two breasts. Look for rabbits weighing 2 to 2½ pounds and they will cook up tender.

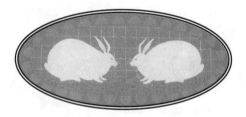

Potted Rabbit

MAKES 4 TO 6 SERVINGS

We often put up visiting marble sculptors from the Carving Studio in West Rutland. For several summers, Inuit carvers have studied marble sculpting at the studio and shared their own art with the community. (They told me how they stored caribou and whale meat by burying it deep in the tundra for winter use.) I served this dish to some visiting Inuit, and they thought it far more delicious than the steak they had had the night before.

Braising rabbit tenderizes the meat and infuses it with the flavors of the aromatic bacon and oregano. Serve over noodles.

3 strips thick bacon
½ cup slivered onions
2 carrots, diced
2 stalks celery, diced
1 teaspoon dried oregano
1 tablespoon olive oil
One 2- to 2½-pound rabbit, skinned and cut into 6 pieces
½ cup all-purpose flour
½ teaspoon salt
¼ teaspoon freshly ground black pepper
½ cup chicken stock (page 2)
½ cup dry white wine

Cut the bacon into ¼-inch-wide strips and cook in a large, heavy-bottomed skillet over medium heat, stirring, until the fat has been rendered but the bacon is not yet crisp, about 5 minutes. Add the vegetables and oregano, cover, and cook for 5 minutes. Remove to a large bowl and set aside.

Heat the oil in the same large skillet over medium heat. Dredge the rabbit pieces in the flour, tapping off any excess, and brown them on all sides. Sprinkle with the salt and pepper and add the reserved bacon-vegetable mixture, the stock, and wine. Bring to a boil, cover the skillet, reduce the heat to medium-low, and cook until the rabbit is very tender, about 40 minutes. Skim any fat from the sauce and serve.

Crisp-Fried Rabbit

Not so many years ago, rabbit was a staple meat served by country cooks. Most recipes for chicken can be adapted to using rabbit, but keep in mind that rabbit is very lean, and when sautéing or frying, remove the breast and saddle meat first to keep them juicy. The buttermilk helps tenderize the meat. I like to serve Red and Green Cabbage Salad (page 140) with this dish.

4 cups fresh buttermilk
One 2- to 2½-pound rabbit, skinned and cut into 6 pieces
1½ tablespoons kosher salt
1 cup all-purpose flour
1 teaspoon freshly ground black pepper
⅔ cup vegetable oil for frying

Pour the buttermilk in a 2-quart bowl. Pat the rabbit pieces dry with a paper towel and sprinkle them with the salt. Place the rabbit in the buttermilk, making sure that all the pieces are submerged. Cover the bowl with plastic wrap and refrigerate overnight.

Place the flour and pepper in a plastic bag. Heat the oil in a large, heavy-bottomed skillet over medium heat until it shimmers. Drain the rabbit pieces and discard the liquid. Place the pieces in the plastic bag and shake to coat them with the flour mixture. Carefully add the rabbit pieces to the oil and fry, turning them occasionally, until golden brown and the breasts and saddles feel tender when pierced with a fork, about 25 minutes. Remove the breast and saddle meat and drain on paper towels. Cover loosely with a sheet of aluminum foil to keep it warm. Cook the legs about 5 minutes longer and drain.

Venison Pepper Steak

Jim Austin, who is no relation to my neighbor Tom, comes from a family that loves to hunt. Their farm lies on top of the hill in the woods across from our house. Last November, Jim's mother was the first to bag a deer. Jim eagerly awaits the last two weeks in November when hunting season occurs. The weather must be cold enough to prevent the meat from spoiling until it can be safely stored in their freezer.

Four 6-ounce venison steaks
1 tablespoon coarsely ground black pepper
½ teaspoon salt
1 tablespoon pure olive oil
1 cup beef stock (page 2)
1 tablespoon balsamic vinegar
1 teaspoon unsalted butter

Place the steaks on a cutting board and make several notches along the fatty outer edges to prevent the meat from curling during cooking. Sprinkle the steaks generously with the pepper and salt on both sides.

Heat the oil in a large, heavy-bottomed skillet over medium-high heat and, for medium-rare, cook the steaks 4 minutes on each side. Remove to a dish and cover loosely with a sheet of aluminum foil to keep the meat warm. Add the stock to the pan and raise the heat to high. Cook the stock until only ½ cup remains. Add the vinegar and any accumulated juices from the steaks and cook for 1 minute. Remove from the heat and swirl in the butter. Pour the sauce over the steaks and serve.

Venison Chops

MAKES 4 TO 6 SERVINGS

Tom Austin, my neighbor in Ira, has been hunting since he was a boy. He also butchers deer meat for friends and has developed this tasty marinade for chops, steaks, and kabobs. He likes to grill them using apple wood chunks soaked in water for half an hour, then added to a slow-burning fire. Look for fallow deer, available from fine butchers, if you are unable to find a hunter willing to share his bounty.

One 12-ounce bottle dark beer
3 tablespoons pure olive oil
¼ cup minced onions
3 cloves garlic, peeled and minced
½ teaspoon salt
½ teaspoon freshly ground black pepper
Juice of 1 lemon
¼ teaspoon dried tarragon leaves
Dash of hot pepper sauce
2 to 2½ pounds venison chops (about 8 small chops)

Combine the beer, oil, onions, garlic, salt, pepper, lemon juice, tarragon, and hot pepper sauce in a large nonreactive bowl and add the venison chops, tossing to coat them well. Cover the bowl with plastic wrap and refrigerate 4 to 8 hours, turning and piercing the meat with a fork several times.

Heat the grill or make a charcoal fire. Drain the marinade into a small saucepan and bring to a boil. Boil for 2 minutes. For medium-rare, grill the chops for 5 minutes on each side, brushing them occasionally with the marinade. Brush the marinade on the cooked side of the chops only, to avoid any contamination from the raw meat. Drizzle any leftover marinade on the chops and serve.

Spicy Venison Chili

While working on *Tomato Imperative!*, I discovered how delicious chipotle chiles are. They lend a rich, smoky flavor when added to sauces, are available dried or canned, and a little goes a long way. My co-author and neighbor, Sharon Nimtz, a very inventive cook, told me how she prepares venison Southwestern style. We actually have a chili cookoff in Fair Haven every year and, wow, do some folks like the hot stuff! This is delicious served over hot rice.

1 tablespoon pure olive oil
1 pound ground venison
1 cup finely chopped onions
2 cloves garlic, peeled and minced
½ teaspoon ground cumin
½ teaspoon ground coriander
¼ teaspoon ground cinnamon
½ teaspoon salt
¼ teaspoon freshly ground black pepper
1 or 2 dried chipotle chiles, soaked in ½ cup boiling water until softened
2 cups canned diced tomatoes
One 15½-ounce can pinto beans, drained and rinsed

Heat the oil in a large skillet over medium heat and brown the venison, breaking up any clumps with a fork. Add the onions, garlic, cumin, coriander, cinnamon, salt, and pepper and cook, stirring occasionally, until the onions are softened, about 10 minutes.

Drain the chiles, reserving the soaking liquid, and chop them finely. Add the chiles to the skillet with the reserved liquid and tomatoes and cook over medium-low heat, uncovered, for 30 minutes. Stir in the beans and cook 10 minutes more.

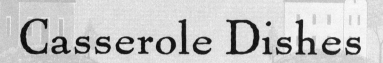

Casserole Dishes

COVERED-DISH SUPPERS ARE potluck and can be the most interesting of all. People like to bring their favorite casseroles and ethnic specialties to these suppers, and it is fun to try a taste of everything.

This summer I attended a potluck supper given in support of the Belmont Historical Museum. People brought not only their covered dishes but their own tableware as well. As Elsie Masterton recounted in *Nothing Whatever to Do* after her husband went back home to get their silverware, "The really coveted covered dishes of the most renowned cooks were scraped clean. But there was enough still, for us . . . We ate silently. Everybody smiled at us, as upperclassmen to freshmen. At a covered-dish supper you brang your own tools. We oughta knowed better."

There is so much variety at these suppers that even a vegetarian has a fighting chance of finding plenty to eat. Usually the person coordinating the supper will telephone and ask for a main dish or a dessert. But some times potluck is just what you get. Eleven different pots of baked beans turned up at one such supper.

One of the first suppers we ever attended was a dime-a-dip supper. In those preinflationary times each scoop of food you took cost a dime. A nice feature of all these suppers is the effort made by the members of the community. The women usually make the food, while the men and children serve the tables. And everyone cleans up!

A casserole means not only a dish in which food is cooked and served, but "casserole" has come to mean the actual dish. A lasagne can qualify as a casserole, as does a shepherd's pie. Many people think of those dreary, overcooked tuna-noodle messes when they hear the word "casserole." Made with fresh ingredients, casseroles can assume front-row status.

Succotash Pie

MAKES 6 TO 8 SERVINGS

Native Americans taught early settlers to make *misickquatash*, a stew of dried corn and beans or peas. It remains a mystery how indigenous peoples discovered healthful food combinations, for corn and beans make a completely available protein. Though the name we know is "succotash" and there have been some changes to the recipe, it remains a true culinary link to the past.

FOR THE SUCCOTASH

1 tablespoon unsalted butter

½ cup coarsely chopped onions

1 cup seeded and diced green bell peppers

2 cups corn kernels

One 10-ounce package frozen baby lima beans, thawed

½ teaspoon dried thyme leaves

½ teaspoon salt

¼ teaspoon freshly ground black pepper

½ cup water

½ cup vegetable stock (page 2)

FOR THE CORNMEAL TOPPING

4 cups water

1 teaspoon salt

1 cup stone-ground cornmeal

½ cup grated Cheddar cheese

Preheat the oven to 425°F. Butter a shallow 3-quart baking dish or casserole. To make the succotash, heat the butter in a medium-size saucepan over medium heat and cook the onions and peppers, stirring occasionally, until the vegetables soften and begin to brown, about 10 minutes. Add the corn, limas, thyme, salt, pepper, and water. Bring to a boil, cover, reduce the heat to medium-low, and cook until the limas are tender, 15 to 20 minutes. Add the stock, adjust the seasonings, pour into the baking dish, and set aside.

To make the cornmeal topping, bring the water and salt to a boil in a medium-size saucepan over medium-high heat. Very slowly sprinkle in the cornmeal while whisking vigorously. Cook, stirring, until very thick, about 10 minutes. Spoon the cornmeal over the bean mixture and sprinkle with the cheese. Bake in the center rack of the oven until lightly browned and bubbling, about 30 minutes. Cool for 10 minutes before serving.

Maggie's Cauliflower Cheese Bake

MAKES 4 TO 6 SERVINGS

At a Belmont potluck supper, I asked who made the delicious cauliflower dish and Maggie Blaine raised her hand. Maggie has spent her summers since childhood in Belmont, a quiet village in the Green Mountains. She told me it was her mother's recipe from the Farmingdale, Long Island, Women's Club cookbook, *That Extra Ingredient*. A touch of aromatic curry powder is the extra ingredient in this adapted version.

1 large cauliflower (about 1½ pounds), cut into florets

3 tablespoons unsalted butter

½ cup chopped onions

1 cup (3 ounces) sliced mushrooms

3 tablespoons all-purpose flour

1 teaspoon curry powder

2 cups milk

1 cup grated sharp Cheddar cheese

½ teaspoon salt

¼ teaspoon freshly ground black pepper

Fresh lemon juice to taste

¼ cup dried bread crumbs

Preheat the oven to 350°F. Butter a 9-inch-deep pie plate. Cook the cauliflower in a large pot of boiling salted water over high heat for 5 minutes. Drain, rinse in cold water, and drain again. Place the cauliflower in the pie plate and set aside.

To make the sauce, heat 2 tablespoons of the butter in a large skillet over medium heat and cook the onions until just softened, about 5 minutes Add the mushrooms and cook, stirring, until softened, about 5 minutes. Sprinkle with the flour and curry powder and stir well. Cook for 2 minutes and stir in the milk. Bring to a boil, reduce the heat to medium-low, and cook for 3 to 4 minutes, or until the sauce has thickened. Remove the skillet from the heat and stir in the cheese, salt, pepper, and lemon juice.

Spoon the sauce over the cauliflower, sprinkle the top with the bread crumbs, and dot with the remaining tablespoon butter. Bake until the crumbs are golden brown and the sauce is bubbling, about 40 minutes.

Gratin of Zucchini and Walnuts

MAKES 6 TO 8 SERVINGS

Gardening can be challenging. Who has not learned to plant fewer zucchini? It is no problem to find ways to use the tender, small zucchini, but what about those baseball bats one finds hidden away under the leaves? One solution is to scoop out the seeds and peel off the skin. The flesh of these huge squashes can then be grated and baked into this enjoyable casserole.

4 cups grated zucchini, seeds and skin removed

½ cup grated onions

1 tablespoon kosher salt

4 large eggs, separated

½ cup all-purpose flour

½ cup freshly grated Parmesan cheese

1 cup coarsely chopped walnuts

¼ teaspoon freshly ground black pepper

1 tablespoon minced fresh parsley leaves

Preheat the oven to 400°F. Butter a 2-quart casserole. Place the zucchini and onions in a colander in the sink and toss with the salt. Set aside for 20 minutes, then squeeze as much liquid from the vegetables as possible. Put the vegetables in a large bowl and stir in the egg yolks, flour, cheese, nuts, pepper, and parsley until well blended.

Beat the egg whites in another large bowl with an electric mixer until softly mounded but not until stiff peaks form. Stir one third of the whites into the zucchini mixture, then fold in the remainder; some white may show. Spoon into the casserole and bake until puffed and brown, 25 to 30 minutes. Serve hot.

Barley and Mushroom–
Stuffed Cabbage

MAKES 6 TO 8 SERVINGS

A hearty dish, not stuffed in the traditional way, it is layered with sautéed cabbage and flavored with dried mushrooms and fresh dill. If you can find dried Chilean mushrooms in the health food store, use them; they are intensely smoky and flavorful. Experiment with other dried mushrooms to find which you prefer. Many varieties are now available in the produce department of my local market.

½ ounce dried mushrooms, soaked for 30 minutes in 1 cup boiling water

3 cups cooked barley

¼ cup unsalted butter

2 cups coarsely chopped onions

4 cups sliced mushrooms

6 cups sliced cabbage

1 teaspoon salt

¼ teaspoon freshly ground black pepper

2 tablespoons chopped fresh dill

Sour cream (optional)

Preheat the oven to 400°F. Butter a 3-quart casserole. Drain the soaked mushrooms through a sieve lined with a paper towel. Reserve the mushroom liquid. Rinse the mushrooms under cold water, blot dry, coarsely chop, and place in a medium-size bowl.

Heat 3 tablespoons of the butter in a large skillet and cook the onions and mushrooms over medium heat until very wilted and beginning to brown, about 15 minutes. Remove half of this mixture to the bowl with the chopped mushrooms. Stir the barley, ½ teaspoon of the salt, and ¼ teaspoon of the pepper into this mixture and set aside.

Add the cabbage to the remaining onion-mushroom mixture in the skillet and cook, stirring, until the cabbage is very wilted, about 20 minutes. Season with the remaining ½ teaspoon salt, ¼ teaspoon pepper, and the dill. Layer one third of the cabbage with half of the mushroom-barley mixture. Repeat the layers, ending with cabbage. Pour the reserved mushroom liquid over the cabbage, dot with the remaining tablespoon butter, and bake for 30 minutes. Serve hot with sour cream if desired.

Hodgepodge

MAKES 4 TO 6 SERVINGS

A random choosing of new vegetables from the garden makes this old country-style dish. The use of salt pork was more common in the past when people kept pigs and salting was one of the few methods of preservation. Look for the meatiest piece of salt pork you can find when making this dish or substitute some meaty bacon. Serve hot with Brown-Bread Muffins (page 128) for an old-fashioned hearty supper that is much appreciated after stacking the wood pile.

3 quarts water
1 tablespoon kosher salt
1 cup 1-inch-thick pieces string beans
1 cup 1-inch-thick slices carrots
2 cups 1-inch-thick pieces unpeeled potatoes
1 cup cauliflower florets
1 cup fresh baby or petite peas (if using frozen, thaw)
1 cup diced salt pork
1 cup heavy cream
1 cup vegetable stock (page 2)
Salt and freshly ground black pepper to taste

continued

Preheat the oven to 425°F. Butter a 3-quart casserole. Bring the water to a boil in a large pot with some salt. Cook the vegetables (except peas if using frozen) in the boiling water for 5 minutes. Drain well.

In a large skillet, cook the salt pork over medium heat until lightly browned, 7 to 8 minutes. Stir in the cream, stock, and vegetables (including the thawed peas) and salt and pepper. Scrape into the casserole and bake until bubbling and lightly browned, 25 to 30 minutes. Serve hot.

COUNTRY TIPS AND TALES

Remember "Waste not, want not," and turn most leftover meat and vegetables into soups by adding some broth and seasoning to taste.

Kale, Tomato, and Bean Casserole

MAKES 6 TO 8 SERVINGS

Kale is one of those dark green leafy vegetables that are so good for us. It is one of the rare vegetables that grows under the snow.

Once I lived in the Ironbound, the Portuguese neighborhood in Newark, New Jersey. The shops sell mounds of finely shredded kale for making their favorite dish, *caldo verde*. This garlicky casserole was inspired by that time and it is often the one dish I bring to potluck or tasting suppers.

¼ cup pure olive oil

3 cloves garlic, peeled and minced

16 cups finely shredded kale leaves, no stems (1 large bunch, about 2 pounds)

3 cups peeled and chopped fresh tomatoes or one 28-ounce can crushed tomatoes

1 teaspoon sweet Hungarian paprika

½ teaspoon salt

¼ teaspoon freshly ground black pepper

One 16-ounce can cannellini beans, drained

½ cup dried bread crumbs

½ cup freshly grated Parmesan cheese

2 tablespoons minced fresh parsley leaves

Preheat the oven to 400°F. Lightly oil a shallow 9 × 13-inch casserole. Heat 2½ tablespoons of the olive oil in a large skillet and cook half the garlic for 1 minute over medium heat. Add the kale and, stirring often, cook until it is wilted, about 5 minutes. Stir in the tomatoes, paprika, salt, and pepper and cook for 5 minutes. Stir in the beans.

Scrape the mixture into the casserole. In a small bowl, combine the remaining 1½ tablespoons olive oil and garlic with the bread crumbs, cheese, and parsley. Sprinkle evenly on top of the vegetables and bake until well browned and bubbling, 25 to 30 minutes. Serve hot, warm, or cold.

North Country Onion Pie

When you think of quiche or *flamiche*, the Alsatian leek tart, onion pie doesn't seem odd at all. Cooked with fresh herbs and sandwiched between two buttery crusts, the onion once again proves its delicious usefulness. This savory pie was probably invented by a cook who looked in her larder for apples and found onions instead.

FOR THE PASTRY

1½ cups all-purpose flour

1 teaspoon salt

Pinch of sugar

6 tablespoons (¾ stick) cold unsalted butter, cut into pieces

¼ cup cold vegetable shortening

2 tablespoons sour cream

2 tablespoons water

FOR THE FILLING

2 tablespoons unsalted butter

8 cups thinly sliced onions

1 tablespoon minced fresh parsley leaves

1 tablespoon minced fresh thyme leaves

2 tablespoons all-purpose flour

¾ teaspoon salt

¼ teaspoon freshly ground black pepper

1 cup milk

To make the crust, stir the flour, salt, and sugar together in a large bowl. Cut in the butter and shortening with a pastry blender or two knives or rub it in with your fingers until the mixture resembles oatmeal. Small lumps of butter may remain. Stir in the sour cream and water with a fork until the dough gathers into a ball. Add more water if needed. Place the dough on a lightly floured worktable and roll the dough with a floured rolling pin into a rectangle about 4 × 6 inches. Fold into thirds like a letter and roll out again to a rectangle. Repeat this procedure once more, then cover the dough with plastic wrap or waxed paper and chill at least 1 hour.

To make the filling, heat the butter in a large skillet over low heat, add the onions, cover, and cook until very tender but not browned, about 40 minutes. Stir in the herbs, flour, salt, and pepper and cook, stirring occasionally, for 3 minutes. Add the milk and bring to a boil. Cook until the mixture is thickened. Let cool.

Preheat the oven to 425°F. To assemble, divide the dough in half. Roll out half of the dough into a 12-inch circle on a lightly floured worktable. Fit it into a 9- or 9½-inch pie plate and spoon in the filling. Roll out the remaining dough into a 12-inch circle and place it over the filling. Trim off the excess dough and crimp the edges with a fork. Cut several steam vents in the top crust. Bake for 15 minutes, reduce the oven temperature to 375°F, and bake until the crust is browned, 20 to 30 minutes. Cool on a rack for 10 minutes before slicing.

COUNTRY TIPS AND TALES

One traditional rhyme goes: "Onions' skins, very thin, mild winter coming in. Onions' skins very tough, winter's coming cold and rough."

Friday Night Smoked-Fish and Potato Dish

MAKES 4 TO 6 SERVINGS

Every Friday was a meatless day when my husband was growing up and his mother made a cod-and-potato dish that he fondly remembers. Smoked cod or haddock layered with onions and potatoes and cooked in cream makes a meal that causes no one to miss the meat.

When made with smoked haddock, the dish is known as "finnan haddie," a delectable Scottish addition to the supper table.

8 ounces smoked cod or haddock fillets
2 tablespoons unsalted butter
1 cup sliced onions
4 large boiling potatoes, peeled and thinly sliced
Salt and freshly ground black pepper to taste
2 cups heavy cream

Preheat the oven to 350°F. Butter a shallow 2-quart baking dish. Crumble the fish, making sure to remove any bones. Heat the butter in a large skillet over medium heat and cook the onions until softened, about 5 minutes. Stir in the fish.

Layer the potatoes, with the onion-fish mixture, sprinkling with salt and pepper. Pour the cream over the top, cover, and bake until the mixture is bubbling and the potatoes tender when pierced with a knife, about 1 hour.

COUNTRY TIPS AND TALES

Drying and smoking fish were common ways of preservation in prerefrigerator times. Old "receipts" called for salt salmon, which needed soaking before it could be cooked. Today we still use salt cod in the same manner.

Savory Green Chile, Corn, and Rice Pudding

MAKES 6 TO 8 SERVINGS

I was making quiches for a friend's night-before-the-wedding supper and some custard filling and Swiss cheese were left over. Looking in the refrigerator to see what else needed using up, I found some cooked corn and leftover brown rice. The serendipitous combination led to this savory pudding spiked with green chiles and cumin.

    4 large eggs
    3 cups milk
    1 teaspoon salt
    ¼ teaspoon freshly ground black pepper
    2 cups corn kernels
    2 cups cooked brown or white rice
    One 4-ounce can diced green chiles
    ½ teaspoon ground cumin
    ½ cup shredded Swiss cheese

Preheat the oven to 350°F. Butter a shallow 3-quart casserole. Beat the eggs with the milk, ½ teaspoon of the salt, and ⅛ teaspoon of the pepper until well combined. Mix the corn, rice, chiles, cumin, and the remaining ½ teaspoon salt and ⅛ teaspoon pepper together in a bowl. Spoon evenly into the casserole and pour the egg mixture on top. Sprinkle with the cheese and bake on the center rack of the oven until the custard is set and the top lightly browned, about 40 minutes.

Grandma's Noodle Kugel

Sadie Cutler, my maternal grandmother, was a wonderful cook who indulged her husband's love of noodles. Every week she made *lukshen* (noodles) in chicken soup or in this baked pudding. It can be made as a dessert, sweetened and full of apples, raisins, and cinnamon, or as a main course, savory with browned onions and poppy seeds, like this version. Sweet or savory, it proves you don't have to be Italian to make pasta.

Homemade noodles are one of the foods kids love to make because making them is such a hands-on experience. The kneading and cutting can be done with a pasta machine if you have one, although the machine only gives one size for cutting noodles and I prefer a wider noodle for this dish.

FOR THE NOODLE DOUGH

2 cups all-purpose flour

2 large eggs

1/8 teaspoon salt

2 to 3 tablespoons water

FOR THE FILLING

2 tablespoons unsalted butter

2 cups coarsely chopped onions

1 cup farmer cheese or small curd cottage cheese

1 cup sour cream

4 large eggs

1 tablespoon poppy seeds

1 teaspoon salt

1/4 teaspoon freshly ground black pepper

To make the noodles, place the flour in a mound on a worktable and make a well in the center. Place the eggs, salt, and water in the well and mix together with a fork, gradually drawing in enough flour to make a kneadable dough. Knead the dough, scraping the work surface and flouring it lightly to prevent sticking, until the dough is smooth and elastic, 5 to 7 minutes. Cover the dough with a clean kitchen towel and let it rest for half an hour.

Cut the dough in half. Roll out each half to a 12 × 16-inch rectangle of dough, less than 1/16 inch thick, using some flour to keep the dough from sticking. Roll up the dough like a jelly roll and cut into 1/2-inch-wide strips. Open up the strips and let dry for 15 minutes on a kitchen towel. Repeat with the remaining dough.

Cook the noodles in a large pot of boiling salted water until al dente, about 3 minutes. Drain and rinse in cold water. Drain again.

Preheat the oven to 425°F. Butter a 2-quart casserole. Heat the butter in a large skillet over medium heat and cook the onions, stirring, until well browned, about 20 minutes. Scrape into a large bowl and stir in the cheese, sour cream, eggs, poppy seeds, salt, and pepper. Stir the noodles into the onion mixture. Spoon into the casserole and bake until the top is lightly browned, about 30 minutes. Let cool for 10 minutes before serving.

COUNTRY TIPS AND TALES

If you eat pudding on the Sabbath, you'll be full all week.
—Leo Rosten's Treasury of Jewish Quotations

Soups and Breads
for Supper

THE WORD "SUPPER" COMES from the Old French *souper*, because to eat soup was to sup. A large pot hung from a hook in the fireplace, which was the cooking and heating source for the house. The housewife would toss all the scraps of vegetables, any bones, and leftovers into the pot for the next meal. Usually flavored with a ham bone, "bean or pease porritch" is often mentioned in old records. We still eat a very similar soup two hundred years later. On cold nights, the hot nourishment of a thick, hearty split pea soup is thoroughly appreciated.

Oyster suppers were fairly common in the past and we went to one of the last, all the way up in the Northeast Kingdom of Vermont. Fresh oysters used to be shipped by train from Rhode Island and were quite the treat. In volume three of *Green Mountain*

Whittlin's, an old man recalled that "The menfolk were served raw oysters, while the ladies ate oyster stew." Today, some families serve oysters in their turkey stuffing, a very old English tradition.

My mother used to joke on the way home from tasting some restaurant's chicken soup, "The chicken just walked through that soup." Learning from her to be a smart cook, I freeze all the backs, wing tips, necks, and giblets (except the liver, which I freeze separately) from chickens until there are 3 to 4 pounds, and then I make a flavorful soup. Don't throw out those bones so you can discover how delicious homemade soups can be.

While my mother taught me to make soup, it was my mother-in-law who taught me to bake bread. Bread making gives me a sense of continuity from generation to generation, because bread is one of our basic foods. Kneading a mound of dough is one of the most satisfying pleasures the kitchen has to offer a cook.

A friend tells me of her daughter living out in Wyoming who makes bread every day with her bread machine. She defends her machine rightly, because at least she is having the best, freshest, most wholesome bread available to her. Perhaps I am old-fashioned, but I love the feel of dough in my hands. Years ago at our restaurant, La Famille, I made forty loaves of bread at a time by hand! I learned by touch to know dough, its changeability and characteristics. Later on, working with commercial mixers, bread baking became easier, but never quite as satisfying.

Baking, unlike cooking, is a regulated affair. While you can be wildly varying in your amounts with a stew with great results, you had better measure carefully if those biscuits and muffins are to come out right. And the strong hand that kneaded the bread must be ever so light when it comes to the tender product wanted in baking powder biscuits. Understanding types of flours, sugars, and yeast and other leavenings and their interplay make baking the most challenging culinary endeavor and the most fun.

Ice-Fish Chowder

MAKES 4 TO 6 SERVINGS

With no sea coast, Vermonters relied on rivers and lakes for their fish. It has been many years since any Vermont fish was available commercially and only those homes with dedicated fishermen and women can count on a local fish for supper. Craig McWaters from Blissville is one such dedicated person. He loves winter because it is ice-fishing season. On many winter days you can find him in a small hut, sitting upon frozen Lake Bomoseen. The lake is dotted with these huts, and some people even drive their trucks out onto the ice. He brings us his extra lake trout and I like to make a supper of traditional fish stew or chowder with it.

    2 ounces meaty salt pork, diced
    1 cup coarsely chopped onions
    2 cups cubed unpeeled boiling potatoes
    2 cups fish stock (page 2) or 1 cup bottled clam broth mixed with
        1 cup water
    2 cups milk
    ¼ teaspoon freshly ground black pepper
    One 2-pound lake trout, cleaned, skinned, and boned, or
        2 cups cubed fish fillets of your choice
    2 teaspoons unsalted butter
    1 tablespoon finely chopped fresh parsley leaves or chives

In a medium-size saucepan, heat the salt pork over medium heat until it renders its fat, about 10 minutes. Add the onions and potatoes and toss to coat with the fat. Cook until the onions are softened, about 5 minutes. Add the fish stock, milk, and pepper, reduce the heat to medium-low, and cook until the potatoes are tender, about 20 minutes. Cut the fish into 1-inch pieces and add to the soup. Adjust the heat to gently cook the soup for another 5 minutes. Adjust the seasoning, swirl in the butter, sprinkle with the parsley, and serve.

Oyster Stew

Oysters used to be considered poor man's food because they were so plentiful. Today they are scarce and the height of elegance, showing how impossible it is to separate food from history and environmental consequences. Now oysters are usually reserved for holidays, but this stew makes a really good supper dish and preserves their briny ocean flavor.

The larches had turned golden as we drove almost to the Canadian border one October to find the Charleston Oyster Supper. For forty years the firemen have served bowls of delectable oyster stew to the surrounding communities of this very rural area. They had to move the supper from the church to the elementary school because the supper became so popular, drawing a crowd of four hundred. I sat with some friendly women; one of them urged me to try her pie, and we ended up exchanging recipes.

1 pint shucked oysters
3 cups milk
1 cup heavy cream
Salt and freshly ground black pepper to taste
Common or oyster crackers

Drain the oysters, reserving the liquid. Make sure there are no bits of shell mixed in with them. Place the oyster liquid, milk, and cream in a medium-size nonreactive saucepan over medium heat and bring to a boil. Add the oysters and bring back to the boil. Remove from the heat and season with salt and pepper. Serve with crackers.

COUNTRY TIPS AND TALES

Common crackers are soda crackers that were sold in barrels at every general store. They are still made in Vermont under the Vermont Common Cracker and the Westminster Cracker labels.

Sweet Pepper and Corn Chowder

Flecked with green and red peppers and made with fresh sweet corn, this soup makes a fine supper with a salad, some cheese, apples, and bread. Of course, you can make the soup with frozen or canned corn but that fresh corn sweetness comes only in summertime.

    4 ears fresh corn, shucked and cooked
    2 tablespoons unsalted butter
    1 medium-size green bell pepper, seeded and diced
    1 medium-size red bell pepper, seeded and diced
    1 cup diced onions
    1 cup diced celery
    1 cup diced unpeeled boiling potatoes
    3 tablespoons all-purpose flour
    3 cups vegetable stock (page 2)
    2 cups milk
    ½ teaspoon salt
    ¼ teaspoon freshly ground black pepper
    1 tablespoon finely chopped fresh parsley leaves

continued

Scrape the corn kernels from the cobs with a sharp knife and set aside. Heat the butter in a 3-quart saucepan over medium heat and cook the peppers, onions, celery, and potatoes, stirring occasionally, until the vegetables are softened but not browned, about 10 minutes. Add the flour, stir together, and cook for 3 minutes. Add the stock, milk, salt, and pepper and bring to a boil. Cook for 3 minutes, reduce the heat to medium-low, add the reserved corn, and cook until the potatoes are tender, about 20 minutes. Adjust the seasoning, sprinkle with the parsley, and serve.

COUNTRY TIPS AND TALES

A picturesque planting maxim was
"Plant your corn when the leaves on the oak trees
are the size of a mouse's ear."

Cream of Parsnip Soup

Root vegetables like parsnips were much more popular in the past. That is a shame because their unique, sweet flavor goes perfectly with many fall and winter dishes. You can vary this soup by adding some carrots or potatoes.

2 tablespoons unsalted butter

½ cup finely chopped onions

2 pounds parsnips, peeled, cored, and diced

3 cups chicken stock (page 2)

½ teaspoon salt (if using canned broth, taste before adding)

¼ teaspoon freshly ground black pepper

¼ cup heavy cream

1 tablespoon finely chopped fresh parsley or chervil leaves

Heat the butter in a large saucepan over medium heat and cook the onions and parsnips, stirring, until the onions soften and begin to brown, about 10 minutes. Add the chicken stock, salt, and pepper and bring to a boil. Cover, reduce the heat to medium-low, and cook until the parsnips are tender, about 30 minutes. Carefully puree the soup through a food mill or in a blender or food processor (you may need to do this in several batches) and return to the soup pot. Add the cream and reheat just until hot. Do not boil. Sprinkle with the parsley and serve.

COUNTRY TIPS AND TALES

When you cut open a parsnip, there is often a tough, woody core. Cut this out and chop the remainder. Parsnips winter over in the garden and get sweeter for it.

Spring Sorrel Soup

MAKES 6 TO 8 SERVINGS

Sorrel, known also as sour grass, has a lemony taste, and is one of the spring greens eaten to restore appetites dulled from the heavy diet of winter. Sorrel is a very hardy perennial, full of vitamins, and when combined with potato makes a soup to long for in April.

2 tablespoons unsalted butter

⅔ cup finely chopped onions

4 cups loosely packed torn sorrel leaves (reserve 5 whole leaves for garnish)

2 pounds boiling potatoes, peeled and cubed

5 cups chicken stock (page 2)

1 teaspoon salt (if using canned broth, taste before adding)

¼ teaspoon freshly ground black pepper

⅔ cup heavy cream

Heat the butter in a 3-quart saucepan over medium heat and cook the onions, stirring, until softened, about 5 minutes. Add the sorrel, potatoes, stock, salt, and pepper and bring to a boil. Cover, reduce the heat to medium-low, and simmer until the potatoes are tender, 30 to 40 minutes. Carefully puree the soup through a food mill or in a blender or food processor (you may need to do this in several batches) and return to the soup pot. Add the cream and reheat. Cut the reserved sorrel leaves into fine shreds. Pour the soup into a tureen, sprinkle with the sorrel shreds, and serve.

COUNTRY TIPS AND TALES

A word of caution: Most soups freeze extremely well except those with potato. Something happens in the freezing that makes the potato texture mealy and unpleasant.

Sweet Pea Soup

MAKES 4 TO 6 SERVINGS

This is as different as can be from the Smoked Ham Hock and Pea Soup (page 110). You can make this delicate soup from fresh sugar snap peas or sweet peas in their pods. No shelling! Just pick off the stems and pull down to the bottom of the pea to remove the strings. Peas are planted early in the spring and you don't have to wait too long before they start producing pea pods so you can make this soup.

2 tablespoons unsalted butter
½ cup finely chopped onions
4 cups (14 ounces) peas in their pods
3 cups chicken stock (page 2)
1 teaspoon salt (if using canned broth, taste before adding)
¼ teaspoon freshly ground black pepper
½ cup heavy cream
1½ tablespoons finely chopped fresh tarragon leaves

Heat the butter in a 3-quart saucepan over medium heat and cook the onions, stirring, until softened, about 5 minutes. Add the peas, chicken stock, salt, and pepper and bring to a boil. Reduce the heat to medium-low and cook, uncovered, until the pods are tender, about 30 minutes. Carefully puree the soup with a food mill or in a blender or food processor (you may need to do this in several batches) and return to the soup pot. Add the cream and tarragon and reheat, but do not boil. Pour into a tureen and serve.

COUNTRY TIPS AND TALES

Je vis de bonne soupe et non de beau langage.
(It is good soup and not fine language that keeps me alive.)
—Molière (1622–1673), *Les Femmes Savantes*

Butternut Squash and Apple Soup

This colorful soup, made throughout the winter months with squash and apples stored in the cold cellar, is also a good first course for a Thanksgiving meal. Matt Beebe, who took my place as cook at Spring Lake Ranch, generously shared his recipe for this satisfying soup. He likes to say he is just a plain cook. True, his soup is straightforward and simple, but its flavor is complex and rich. For spicy variation, he adds some fragrant curry powder.

One 2-pound butternut squash, cut in half and seeded
2 tablespoons unsalted butter
½ cup finely chopped onions
½ cup finely diced carrots
½ cup finely diced celery
2 apples, such as Cortland or MacIntosh, unpeeled, cored,
    and coarsely chopped
4 cups vegetable or chicken stock (page 2)
1 teaspoon salt (if using canned broth, taste before adding)
¼ teaspoon freshly ground black pepper
Crème fraîche (page 3)

Preheat the oven to 400°F. Grease a baking sheet. Place the squash cut side down on the baking sheet and cook until it is tender when pierced with a fork, about 1 hour. Remove from the oven and let cool. Peel the skin from the squash and cut the flesh into chunks. Set aside.

Heat the butter in a 3-quart saucepan over medium heat and cook the onions, carrots, celery, and apples, stirring occasionally, until very tender, about 15 minutes. Add the squash, stock, salt, and pepper and bring to a boil. Reduce the heat to medium-low and cook for 40 minutes. Carefully puree the soup through a food mill or in a blender or food processor (you may need to do this in several batches) and return to the saucepan to reheat. Serve in a warmed tureen with a dollop of crème fraîche.

Grandma's Potato Soup

MAKES 6 TO 8 SERVINGS

My grandmother Sadie Cutler was a fine cook, whose expression,
"You put in good, it comes out good," has become a family credo.
This robust potato soup was served during the 1940s to 1960s, as part of
her hearty dairy supper at the Central Hotel in Sharon Springs, New
York, where the mountain air gave her guests keen appetites.

2 tablespoons unsalted butter

1 cup coarsely chopped onions

1 cup coarsely chopped carrots

1 cup coarsely chopped celery

2 cups peeled and cubed boiling potatoes

3 cups milk

1 cup water

1 teaspoon salt

¼ teaspoon freshly ground black pepper

1 tablespoon finely chopped fresh dill

1 tablespoon finely chopped fresh parsley leaves

Heat the butter in a large saucepan over medium heat and cook the onions, carrots, and celery, stirring occasionally, until they begin to brown, about 15 minutes. Add

the potatoes, milk, water, salt, and pepper, reduce the heat to medium-low, and cook until the vegetables are tender, about 40 minutes. Mash some of the potatoes against the side of the saucepan to thicken the soup. Sprinkle with the dill and parsley and serve.

COUNTRY TIPS AND TALES

In a report to the Vermont Board of Agriculture in 1877, a Mr. H. Blake spoke on "Fifty years of Farm Life in Northern Vermont, and Its Lessons." He told of the presence of spirits, including potato whiskey, in the Vermont of the early 1800s: "Spirit of some form was upon the breakfast table, carried into the field at eleven o'clock, at every training, raising, husking, log rolling bee, and sheep washing."

All-of-the-Beet Borscht

MAKES 8 TO 10 SERVINGS

One time when I was making borscht, I threw the beet tops in the soup and discovered how well they worked. As an added bonus, I did not have the greens hanging around wilting in the vegetable drawer, waiting for another use.

There are probably as many versions of this soup as there are Poles, Russians, and Ukrainians. My grandma served hers cold in the summer stirred with sour cream, making a shockingly fuchsia-colored soup. This one is a hot soup based on beef stock.

2 pounds beets with greens, thoroughly washed

2 cups coarsely chopped green cabbage

1 cup coarsely chopped carrots

1 cup coarsely chopped onions

1 cup canned diced tomatoes (undrained)

1 bay leaf

½ cup finely chopped fresh dill

6 cups beef stock (page 2)

6 cups water

1 tablespoon salt (if using canned broth, taste before adding)

¼ teaspoon freshly ground black pepper

½ cup sugar, or more to taste

⅔ cup fresh lemon juice or cider vinegar, or more to taste

FOR GARNISH

8 hot whole boiled potatoes, peeled

Sour cream

Remove the beet greens from the beets and coarsely chop the leaves and stems. Peel and cube the beets. Put all the vegetables, the bay leaf, ¼ cup of the dill, the beef stock, water, salt, and pepper in a deep, nonreactive soup kettle. Bring to a boil over medium heat. Cover, reduce the heat to medium-low, and cook the soup until the beets are tender, about 40 minutes. Uncover and stir in the sugar and lemon juice, adding more of each to balance the flavor, if needed. Stir in the remaining ¼ cup dill and serve in deep soup plates with a potato and a dollop of sour cream.

COUNTRY TIPS AND TALES

Borscht and bread make your cheeks red.

—*Leo Rosten's Treasury of Jewish Quotations*

Savory Bean Soup

MAKES 6 TO 8 SERVINGS

Dried beans played a big role in early kitchens, and today, nutritionists urge us to eat them not only for their protein content, but their fiber content as well. Almost any bean will do for this soup and often more than one bean at that. Soak the beans overnight to save time the next day.

1 cup coarsely chopped onions

1 cup coarsely chopped celery

1 clove garlic, minced

2 cups dried soldier beans, soaked in water to cover overnight and drained

5 cups vegetable stock (page 2) or water

1 bay leaf

½ teaspoon dried savory

½ teaspoon dried thyme leaves

½ teaspoon dried marjoram

2 tablespoons cider vinegar

1 teaspoon salt

¼ teaspoon freshly ground black pepper

FOR GARNISH

1 tablespoon finely chopped fresh parsley leaves

1 tablespoon finely chopped fresh chives

Place the onions, celery, garlic, beans, stock, and dried herbs in a deep soup kettle and bring to a boil over medium heat. Cover, reduce the heat to medium-low, and cook until the beans are tender, about 1½ hours.

Remove 2 cups of the beans and puree with a food mill or in a blender or food processor. Return the puree to the pot. Add the vinegar, salt, and pepper. Pour into a tureen and garnish with the parsley and chives.

COUNTRY TIPS AND TALES

Adding a spoonful of vinegar or citrus juice to a bean or pea soup enlivens the flavor.

Italian Green Bean Soup

MAKES 6 TO 8 SERVINGS

The labor movement owes much to the early Italian immigrants of Vermont. Working in the marble and granite industries, they developed social organizations to care for the families of disabled quarry workers. There are still many people, like Claire Tortolano from Rutland, who remember the close-knit communities of their youth. Claire's grandmother used to remind her shy granddaughter, "*La capo che non parla si chiama cocuzza,*" which means, "A head that doesn't talk is a squash."

When the green beans get past the slender and tender stage, make this flavorful soup, which takes a nod from minestrone. I often serve it with freshly grated Parmesan cheese and sometimes put in cooked pasta at the end.

1 tablespoon olive oil

1 cup coarsely chopped onions

1 clove garlic, peeled and minced

½ pound green beans, cut into ½-inch pieces

1 cup diced fresh or canned tomatoes (undrained)

3 cups chicken or vegetable stock (page 2)

½ teaspoon dried marjoram or savory

1 teaspoon salt (if using canned broth, taste before adding)

¼ teaspoon freshly ground black pepper

Freshly grated Parmesan cheese

Heat the oil in a large saucepan over medium heat and cook the onions and garlic, stirring, until softened, about 5 minutes. Add the beans, tomatoes, stock, marjoram, salt, and pepper and bring to a boil. Reduce the heat to medium-low and cook, stirring occasionally, until the beans are tender, 20 to 25 minutes. Serve, passing the cheese separately.

Muriel's Chicken Soup
with Kreplach

Many cultures have their stuffed dumplings, from wontons to raviolis to kreplach. My mother has always shared her love of cooking with me, and as I watched her use her mother's knife and smooth rolling pin to make the dough for kreplach, I realized the connections, once more, between food and culture.

Measuring the water for the dough in half of the empty egg shell, she showed me how to know the proper consistency of the dough. You can make kreplach ahead and freeze them, but thaw before cooking them in the water.

FOR THE MEAT FILLING

¼ cup vegetable oil

2 cups finely chopped onions

2 cups minced cooked beef (I always use leftover pot roast)

½ teaspoon salt

¼ teaspoon freshly ground black pepper

1 large egg, beaten

FOR THE KREPLACH DOUGH

2 cups all-purpose flour

2 large eggs

⅛ teaspoon salt

3 to 4 tablespoons water

FOR THE SOUP AND TO COOK THE KREPLACH

4 cups chicken stock (page 2), well seasoned

3 quarts water

1 tablespoon kosher salt

1 tablespoon minced fresh parsley leaves

To make the filling, heat the oil in a large skillet and cook the onions, stirring, over medium heat until softened, about 5 minutes. Add the meat and cook, stirring, until the mixture is very dry and well browned, 15 to 20 minutes. Stir often, scraping up the bits that stick to the pan. Cool completely, then stir in the salt, pepper, and egg.

To make the noodles, place the flour in a mound on a work surface and make a well in the center. Place the eggs, salt, and water in the well and mix together with a fork, gradually drawing in enough flour to make a kneadable dough. Knead the dough, scraping the work surface and flouring it lightly to prevent sticking, until it is smooth and elastic, 5 to 7 minutes. Cover the dough with a clean kitchen towel and let it rest for half an hour.

Cut the dough in half. Roll out each half into an 11 × 13-inch rectangle of dough, using some flour to keep the dough from sticking. Cut the dough into 2½-inch squares.

Place a scant teaspoon of the filling in the center of each square. Moisten two adjoining edges of each square with water and fold into a triangle, pinching the edges tightly to seal. Place the filled kreplach on a floured kitchen towel and continue with the remaining dough. You should be able to make 54 to 55 kreplach. Cut any dough scraps into noodles.

Heat the chicken stock in a large pot over medium heat. In a separate large pot, bring the water and salt to a boil and cook the kreplach, stirring occasionally, for 8 to 10 minutes. They should be cooked al dente. Drain, add the kreplach to the hot chicken stock, sprinkle with the parsley, and serve.

Smoked Ham Hock
and Pea Soup

This recipe uses yellow split peas, but green peas or any kind of lentil will also make an excellent soup. This old recipe has many origins, such as the Dutch soup *snert* and the French-Canadian *potée*. It is a type of "bean porritch" found in old histories of colonial settlements.

The old children's taunt, "Pea soup and johnny cake will make a Frenchman's belly ache," won't keep us from enjoying this comfort soup of soups.

1 smoked ham hock

1 cup coarsely chopped onions

1 cup coarsely chopped carrots

1 cup coarsely chopped celery

2 cups dried yellow split peas, picked over and rinsed

1 teaspoon dried thyme leaves

1 bay leaf

6 cups water

1 teaspoon salt

¼ teaspoon freshly ground black pepper

Place all the ingredients in a deep soup kettle and bring to a boil over medium heat. Cover, reduce the heat to low, and cook for 1½ hours. Remove the hock and, when cool enough to handle, pull off any meat and cut into small pieces. Return the meat to the soup, discarding the bone. Discard the bay leaf. Serve hot with buttered Rye-Onion-Walnut Rolls (page 118).

COUNTRY TIPS AND TALES

When you need a smoky flavor and don't want to buy a ham, get a hock. Just one flavors a whole pot of soup.

Rob's Raisin Whole-Wheat Bread

MAKES 2 LOAVES

My co-chef at Spring Lake Ranch was Rob McKain, who is a fine baker. His whole-wheat breads are hearty, never heavy. He uses extra gluten to help lift the dense whole wheat and soaks the raisins so they stay moist. This bread disappears as soon as it is served. Vary this bread with golden raisins, dried cranberries, or a mixture of both.

1½ cups raisins

2½ cups boiling water

3 tablespoons pure dark amber or grade B maple syrup or unsulfured molasses

2 tablespoons (2 envelopes) dry yeast

About 7 cups whole-wheat flour

3 tablespoons pure gluten (available in health food stores under the Vital Wheat Gluten label)

2 teaspoons ground cinnamon

2 teaspoons salt

3 tablespoons unsalted butter, at room temperature

Place the raisins in a large bowl, cover with the boiling water, and let plump for 20 minutes. Stir in the maple syrup and yeast and let sit until bubbly, about 5 minutes. Stir 3 cups of the whole-wheat flour, the gluten, cinnamon, and salt into the bowl and mix well. Cover with a clean kitchen towel, place in a warm place, and let proof for half an hour. It will rise and look frothy.

With a wooden spoon, stir in 2 more cups of the whole-wheat flour to make a soft dough. Use some of the remaining flour to flour the worktable. Place the dough on the surface and knead, adding additional flour to keep it from sticking. Keep flouring your hands. Kneading is done by pushing the dough away from you with the heels of your hands, folding the dough over on itself, turning it, then repeating the pushing, folding, and turning movements until the dough feels elastic and smooth. Usually this takes 8 to 10 minutes. (If any raisins pop out during kneading, just push them back into the dough.) Flatten the dough into a circle and spread with the butter. Fold the dough over the butter and knead about 10 more times. It is fine if some butter shows.

(Alternatively, knead the dough with an electric mixer with a dough hook, adding the flour. When the dough cleans the sides of the bowl, stop adding flour and knead in the butter.)

Place the dough in a large bowl, sprinkle it with a little flour, cover with a clean kitchen towel, and set in a warm, draft-free place to rise until doubled in volume, about 1½ hours.

Grease two 9 × 5-inch loaf pans. Place the dough on a lightly floured worktable and pat firmly into a large rectangle, punching out all the air. Cut in half and fold each piece into thirds like a letter, and roll tightly from the short end like a jelly roll. Pinch the seam shut and place seam down, tucking under the ends, into the loaf pans. Cover with the kitchen towel and let the loaves rise until doubled, about 45 minutes.

Preheat the oven to 350°F. Bake until the loaves are browned and sound hollow when rapped on the bottom, 30 to 40 minutes. Remove the loaves from the pans and cool on a rack before slicing. This bread freezes for up to 1 month when completely cooled and well wrapped in plastic wrap.

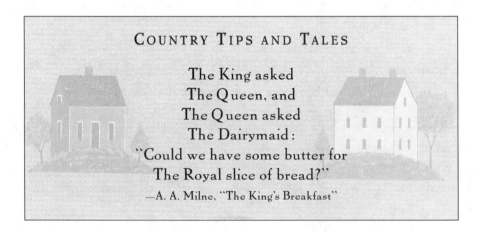

COUNTRY TIPS AND TALES

The King asked
The Queen, and
The Queen asked
The Dairymaid:
"Could we have some butter for
The Royal slice of bread?"
—A. A. Milne, "The King's Breakfast"

My Half-Whole-Wheat
Italian Loaves

MAKES 2 BAGUETTES OR LONG LOAVES

Twenty years ago, our family moved to Vermont from New York City, and one of the things we missed was good bread. I developed this recipe for our restaurant, La Famille, and have been baking it ever since. There are now wonderfully crusty loaves being made by innovative bakers all over the state, but I enjoy baking and when there is time, I do.

1 tablespoon (1 envelope) dry yeast

1 tablespoon honey

2 cups warm water (about 115°F)

2½ cups all-purpose flour and 2½ cups coarsely ground whole-wheat flour, mixed together

¾ cup semolina (available in health food stores)

1 tablespoon salt

Cornmeal for sprinkling

Cold water for brushing the loaves

Place the yeast, honey, and ½ cup of the water in the bowl of an electric mixer fitted with a dough hook and stir to combine. Let sit 5 minutes, until bubbly. Mix in 4 cups of the flours, the semolina, salt, and the remaining 1½ cups water and knead with the machine on slow speed. Add the remaining cup flour and knead until a dough forms and cleans the sides of the bowl. The dough should be soft but not sticky and feel elastic to the touch.

If making by hand, stir 4 cups of the flour, the semolina, salt, and the remaining water into the yeast mixture with a wooden spoon, turn out onto a well-floured worktable, and knead, adding additional flour until the dough cleans the surface, is soft but not sticky, and feels elastic to the touch, 8 to 10 minutes. (Kneading is done by pushing the dough away from you with the heels of your hands, folding the dough over onto itself, turning it, then repeating the pushing, folding, and turning movements until the dough is elastic and smooth.)

continued

Place the dough in a large bowl. Sprinkle it with a little flour, cover the bowl with a clean kitchen towel, and let rise in a warm, draft-free place until doubled in volume, about 1 hour.

Grease a baking sheet and sprinkle with cornmeal or semolina. Punch the air out of the dough and turn it onto a floured worktable. Divide the dough in half, pat each piece into a rectangle, and tightly roll it up like a jelly roll. Pinch the seam closed. With floured hands, roll each of them into a baguette about 16 inches long by pushing it against the table while rolling it. Place the baguettes several inches apart on the sheet and cover with the kitchen towel.

Preheat the oven to 375°F. Let the loaves rise until doubled, 30 to 40 minutes. Slash the tops with a razor blade in three long diagonal slashes. Let rise 10 minutes longer, uncovered. Brush the tops with cold water and bake until well browned and the loaves sound hollow when rapped on the bottom, 20 to 25 minutes. Remove from the pan and cool on a rack before slicing. Baguettes may be frozen for up to 1 month when completely cooled and well wrapped in plastic wrap. Heat thawed, unwrapped bread in a preheated 350°F oven before serving to bring out the flavor.

Maple Oatmeal Bread

MAKES 2 LOAVES

Faced with a pot of leftover cooked oatmeal that my frugal self could not in good conscience throw out, I decided to try making it into a loaf of bread. Soon I was cooking extra cereal just to make these loaves; do not use the quick-cooking type of oats. Also try making the bread with Wheatena or any cooked cereal.

3¼ cup old-fashioned rolled oats
1½ cups boiling water
½ cup pure dark amber or grade B maple syrup
1 cup warm milk (about 115°F)
2 tablespoons (2 envelopes) dry yeast
6 to 7 cups all-purpose flour
1 tablespoon salt
Milk for brushing the loaves

Cook the oats in the boiling water in a small saucepan over medium heat until thickened, about 5 minutes. Scrape the oatmeal into the bowl of an electric mixer fitted with a dough hook and stir in the maple syrup and warm milk. Stir in the yeast and let sit until the mixture is bubbly, about 5 minutes. Mix in 5 cups of the flour and the salt and knead with the machine on slow speed. Add the remaining flour gradually until a dough forms and cleans the sides of the bowl. The dough should be soft but not sticky and feel elastic to the touch.

If making by hand, stir 5 cups of the flour into the oatmeal-yeast mixture with a wooden spoon, turn the dough out onto a well-floured worktable, and knead, using the remaining flour until the dough cleans the surface, is soft but not sticky, and feels elastic to the touch, 8 to 10 minutes. (Kneading is done by pushing the dough away from you with the heels of your hands, folding the dough over onto itself, turning it, then repeating the pushing, folding, and turning movements until the dough is elastic and smooth.)

Place the dough in a large bowl. Sprinkle it with a little flour, cover the bowl with a clean kitchen towel, and let rise in a warm, draft-free place until doubled in volume, about 1 hour.

Grease two 9 × 5-inch loaf pans. Punch the air out of the dough and turn it onto a floured worktable. Divide the dough in half and pat each piece into a rectangle. Fold each into thirds like a letter, then pat out into a rectangle again. Roll up from the short end like a jelly roll. Pinch the seam closed. Place each loaf seam down, tucking the ends under, into the loaf pan and cover with the kitchen towel.

Preheat the oven to 375°F. Let the loaves rise until doubled, about 45 minutes to 1½ hours, depending on the warmth of the kitchen. Brush their tops with the milk.

Bake until well browned and the loaves sound hollow when rapped on the bottom, 30 to 40 minutes. Remove the loaves from the pans and cool on a rack before slicing. This bread freezes for up to 1 month when completely cooled and well wrapped in plastic wrap.

COUNTRY TIPS AND TALES

It's a sign of bad luck if a woman burns bread,
she might be mad all day.
—Ferne Sheton, *Pioneer Superstitions*

Buttermilk Bread

MAKES 2 LOAVES

This is a basic recipe for good sandwich bread that can be varied by substituting 1 to 2 cups of whole-wheat flour for the same amount of white flour. It also makes excellent rolls.

1½ tablespoons (1½ envelopes) dry yeast
1 tablespoon honey
2 cups warm buttermilk (about 115°F)
6 to 7 cups all-purpose flour
1 tablespoon salt
2 tablespoons unsalted butter, melted

Place the yeast, honey, and ½ cup of the buttermilk in the bowl of an electric mixer fitted with a dough hook and stir to combine. Let sit 5 minutes until bubbly. Mix in 5 cups of the flour, the salt, and the remaining buttermilk and knead with the machine on slow speed. Add the remaining flour gradually until a dough forms and cleans the sides of the bowl. The dough should be soft but not sticky and feel elastic to the touch.

If making by hand, stir the flour into the yeast mixture with a wooden spoon, turn the dough out onto a well-floured worktable, and knead, adding more flour until the dough cleans the table, is soft but not sticky, and feels elastic to the touch, 8 to 10 minutes. (Kneading is done by pushing the dough away from you with the heels of your hands, folding the dough over onto itself, turning it, then repeating the pushing, folding, and turning movements until the dough is elastic and smooth.)

Place the dough in a large bowl. Sprinkle it with some flour, cover the bowl with a clean kitchen towel, and let rise in a warm, draft-free place until doubled in volume, about 1 hour.

Grease two 9 × 5-inch loaf pans. Punch the air out of the dough and turn it onto a floured worktable. Cut the dough in half and pat each piece into a rectangle. Fold each into thirds like a letter, then pat out into a rectangle again. Roll up tightly from the short end like a jelly roll. Pinch the seam closed. Place each loaf seam down, tucking the ends under, into the loaf pan and cover with the kitchen towel.

Preheat the oven to 375°F. Let the loaves rise until doubled, 45 to 60 minutes, depending on the kitchen temperature. Brush their tops with the melted butter. Bake until well browned and the loaves sound hollow when rapped on the bottom, 30 to 40 minutes. Remove the loaves from the pans and cool on a rack before slicing. This bread freezes for up to 1 month when completely cooled and well wrapped in plastic wrap.

COUNTRY TIPS AND TALES

Making bread is a great activity to share with children. You can teach a child to appreciate food by involving him or her in the process, and besides, it's fun kneading all that squooshy dough! It is a terrific activity when the weather is stormy.

Rye~Onion~Walnut Rolls

MAKES 2 DOZEN ROLLS

Every holiday season, I make these savory rolls into loaves to give as gifts. After all the sweets, these are a nice change. Cheese goes especially well with them. These were inspired by Jane Grigson from her book *Good Things*.

2 tablespoons (2 envelopes) dry yeast

2 tablespoons honey

2 cups warm milk (about 115°F)

5 cups all-purpose flour

1 cup rye flour

1 tablespoon salt

½ teaspoon freshly ground black pepper

½ cup olive oil

¾ cup chopped onions

¾ cup coarsely chopped walnuts

Place the yeast, honey, and ½ cup of the milk in the bowl of an electric mixer fitted with a dough hook and stir to combine. Let sit 5 minutes, until bubbly. Mix in 4 cups of the all-purpose flour and the rye flour, salt, pepper, olive oil, and the remaining 1½ cups milk and knead with the machine on slow speed. Add the remaining cup flour gradually until a dough forms and cleans the sides of the bowl. Knead in the onions and walnuts. The dough should be soft but not sticky and feel elastic to the touch.

If making by hand, stir the flour into the yeast mixture with a wooden spoon, turn the dough out onto a well-floured worktable, and knead, adding additional flour until the dough cleans the table, is soft but not sticky, and feels elastic to the touch, 8 to 10 minutes. Knead in the onions and walnuts. This feels awkward and lumpy, but keep kneading about 2 minutes. (Kneading is done by pushing the dough away from you with the heels of your hands, folding the dough over onto itself, turning it, then repeating the pushing, folding, and turning movements until the dough is elastic and smooth.)

Place the dough in a large bowl. Sprinkle it with a little flour, cover the bowl with a clean kitchen towel, and let rise in a warm, draft-free place until doubled in volume, about 1 hour.

Grease a baking sheet. Punch the air out of the dough and turn onto a floured work surface. Divide the dough into 24 even pieces and make a ball out of each one by cupping a hand over the dough and pushing it against the table while rolling it. Place the rolls on the baking sheet, leaving 1 inch between each one, and cover with the kitchen towel. Let the rolls rise until doubled, about 30 minutes.

Preheat the oven to 375°F. Bake until well browned and the rolls sound hollow when rapped on the bottom, about 20 minutes. Cool on a rack at least 20 minutes before serving. Rolls can be frozen for up to 1 month when completely cooled and well wrapped. Warm thawed frozen rolls before serving to bring out their flavor.

Orange Pumpkin Rolls

Featherlight and fragrant with orange, these rolls make a welcome addition to a winter supper. The dough will be sticky and I recommend using an electric mixer for the job. Resist adding any additional flour and your results will be perfect.

½ cup milk
3 tablespoons unsalted butter
1½ tablespoons (1½ envelopes) dry yeast
2 tablespoons honey
5½ cups all-purpose flour
1 tablespoon salt
½ cup fresh or canned pumpkin puree
3 large eggs
Juice and grated rind of 1 large orange

Heat the milk and butter together in a small saucepan over low heat until the temperature reaches about 115°F. Place the milk mixture, yeast, and honey in the bowl of an electric mixer fitted with a dough hook and stir to combine. Let sit for 5 minutes until bubbly. Add 5 cups of the flour, the salt, pumpkin, eggs, and orange juice and rind and knead with the machine on slow speed until the dough is elastic, about 5 minutes. It will be sticky, but will form a ball and somewhat clean the sides of the bowl. Remove the bowl from the mixer and sprinkle the dough with the remaining ½ cup flour. Cover the bowl with a clean kitchen towel and let rise in a warm, draft-free place until doubled in volume, about 1 hour.

Grease a baking sheet. Scrape the dough onto a well-floured worktable and knead 4 to 5 times. Cut the dough into 24 even pieces and make a ball out of each piece by cupping a hand over the dough and pushing it against the table while rolling it. Place the rolls on the baking sheet, leaving 1 inch between each roll, and cover with the kitchen towel.

Preheat the oven to 375°F. Let the rolls rise until doubled, about 30 minutes, then bake until well browned and the rolls sound hollow when rapped on the bottom, about

20 minutes. Cool on a rack at least 20 minutes before serving. Rolls can be frozen for up to 1 month when completely cooled and well wrapped. Warm thawed frozen rolls before serving to bring out their flavor.

Nutted Squash Drop Biscuits

MAKES 2 DOZEN

The flavor of hazelnuts intensifies when toasted and complements the sweet squash or pumpkin. These are a great accompaniment to turkey or ham dishes or just served with butter and honey.

1 cup coarsely chopped hazelnuts

2 cups all-purpose flour

2 tablespoons firmly packed light brown sugar

2 teaspoons baking powder

½ teaspoon baking soda

¼ teaspoon salt

3 tablespoons cold unsalted butter, cut into pieces

3 tablespoons cold vegetable shortening

1 cup fresh or canned pumpkin or winter squash puree

¼ cup milk

Preheat the oven to 350°F. Spread the hazelnuts on a baking sheet and toast until light brown and fragrant, about 8 minutes. Watch carefully, as they can burn easily. Cool the nuts.

continued

Raise the oven temperature to 400°F. Grease a baking sheet. Place the hazelnuts, flour, sugar, baking powder and soda, and salt in a large bowl and cut in the butter and shortening with a pastry blender or rub it in with your fingers until the mixture resembles oatmeal. Stir in the pumpkin and milk with a fork until a soft dough forms. Drop the dough by rounded spoonfuls onto the baking sheet about 1 inch apart and bake until golden brown, about 15 minutes. Let rest for 5 minutes before serving.

COUNTRY TIPS AND TALES

Hazelnuts are also called filberts and like all nuts should be stored in the freezer to keep them fresh.
A funny old saying is "Just because the cat had her kittens in the oven doesn't mean they're biscuits."

Dried-Apple Biscuits

MAKES 12 BISCUITS

Make this a triple apple day by serving these very light and tender biscuits with apple cider jelly and sweet butter.

1 cup diced dried apples (available in health food stores or
   in some supermarket produce sections)
½ cup apple cider
2 cups all-purpose flour
2 tablespoons firmly packed light brown sugar
2 teaspoons baking powder
½ teaspoon baking soda
½ teaspoon salt
¼ teaspoon freshly grated nutmeg
6 tablespoons (¾ stick) cold unsalted butter, cut into pieces
3 tablespoons cold vegetable shortening
⅓ cup buttermilk

Preheat the oven to 400°F. Grease a baking sheet. Plump the dried apples by soaking them in the apple cider for 30 minutes. Place the flour, sugar, baking powder and soda, salt, and nutmeg in a large bowl and cut in the butter and shortening with a pastry blender or two knives or rub it in with your fingers until the mixture resembles oatmeal. Stir in the soaked apples, their liquid, and the buttermilk with a fork until a dough forms. Turn the dough out onto a well-floured worktable and sprinkle with flour. Pat the dough into a 6 × 8-inch rectangle and with a knife dipped in flour, cut into twelve 2-inch squares. Place the squares on the baking sheet about 1 inch apart and bake until golden brown, about 15 minutes. Let rest for 5 minutes before serving.

COUNTRY TIPS AND TALES

Drying apples was a common method of preserving the autumn harvest, and cooks made pies from the dried apples all winter long. Sometimes you can find only dried apple rings. Snip them into pieces with kitchen shears dipped in vegetable oil.

Little Leek Biscuits

MAKES 34 ONE-INCH BISCUITS

Another of the onion family is the leek, with a mellow flavor all its own. Leeks must be washed thoroughly before using to remove any dirt hiding amid their many leaves and tucked into the multiple layers of its bulb.

These buttery little biscuits are delicious with soups and salads.

6 tablespoons (¾ stick) cold unsalted butter

1½ cups finely chopped leeks, white and pale green parts only

2 cups all-purpose flour

2½ teaspoons baking powder

½ teaspoon baking soda

½ teaspoon salt

¾ cup sour cream mixed with ¼ cup water

Preheat the oven to 400°F. Heat 3 tablespoons of the butter in a large skillet over medium-high heat and cook the leeks, stirring, until browned, 5 to 7 minutes. Cool completely.

Place the flour, baking powder and soda, and salt in a large bowl and cut in the remaining butter with a pastry blender or rub it in with your fingers until the mixture resembles oatmeal. With a fork, stir in the leeks and sour cream mixture until a dough forms into a ball.

Scrape the dough onto a well-floured worktable and knead lightly 10 times. Sprinkle the dough with flour and with a floured rolling pin roll out to ½ inch thick. Cut into rounds with a 1-inch cutter. Gently reroll the dough scraps and cut out more rounds. Place the rounds on an ungreased cookie sheet and bake until browned, 15 to 20 minutes. Cool at least 10 minutes before serving.

COUNTRY TIPS AND TALES

The secret to light biscuits is to handle the dough as little as possible. "If it were done where 'tis done then 'twere well It were done quickly."
—Marthas Vineyard Hospital, *Island Cook Book*

Toasted-Oat Gems

MAKES 12 GEMS

Across between a biscuit and a muffin, these tender puffs of oats have lots of flavor; do not use the quick-cooking type of oat. I make them in a shallow tartlet pan but a muffin tin will work just as well. They are good with ham and cheese or Strawberry Rhubarb Preserves (page 204) and cream. These can be toasted for breakfast if you have any left over.

1 cup old-fashioned rolled oats

1 cup all-purpose flour

1 tablespoon firmly packed light brown sugar

2 teaspoons baking powder

½ teaspoon baking soda

½ teaspoon salt

2 tablespoons cold unsalted butter, cut into pieces

2 tablespoons cold vegetable shortening

1 cup buttermilk

Preheat the oven to 400°F. Grease a muffin tin or tartlet pan. Spread the oats on a baking sheet and toast in the oven until lightly colored, about 10 minutes. Cool and grind to a powder in a blender or food processor.

Stir together the oats, flour, sugar, baking powder and soda, and salt in a large bowl. Cut in the butter and shortening with a pastry blender or two knives or rub it in with your fingers until the mixture resembles oatmeal. Stir in the buttermilk with a fork until a very soft dough forms. Spoon into the tin or pan and bake on the center rack of the oven until golden brown, about 20 minutes. Cool for 3 minutes, then remove from the tin to cool on a rack for 10 minutes before serving.

> ### COUNTRY TIPS AND TALES
>
> Oat cakes originated in Scotland and early recipes contained no sugar. In those days a cook built her reputation on the delicacy of her cakes and was known to have a "light hand."

Blueberry Buttermilk Muffins

MAKES 12 MUFFINS

We grow big, juicy blueberries on the hill behind our house and freeze them for the winter to use in making cobblers, cakes, and these muffins. Use frozen whole berries without thawing them. Try serving them with maple cream or butter sweetened with some maple syrup.

1 cup all-purpose flour

1 cup whole-wheat flour

½ cup firmly packed light brown sugar

2 teaspoons baking powder

1 teaspoon baking soda

½ teaspoon salt

½ teaspoon freshly grated nutmeg

2 large eggs

¼ cup vegetable oil

1 cup buttermilk

2 cups fresh or frozen blueberries

Preheat the oven to 375°F. Grease a muffin tin. Stir all the dry ingredients together in a large bowl. In a large bowl, beat the eggs, oil, and buttermilk together with a whisk until well blended. Stir the wet mixture into the dry just until the dry ingredients are moistened. Fold in the blueberries. Spoon into the muffin tin and bake until well puffed and browned and firm to the touch, about 25 minutes. Let cool for 3 minutes and they will be easy to remove from the tin.

COUNTRY TIPS AND TALES

The secret to tender muffins is to stir the batter only enough to moisten the dry ingredients. Resist the urge to stir any more, or else you'll end up with a tough muffin.

Cheddar Muffins

MAKES 12 MUFFINS

Alittle bit of Parmesan brings out the Cheddar flavor. Try these with Savory Bean Soup (page 104) for a satisfying supper.

2 cups all-purpose flour

½ cup cornmeal

2 teaspoons baking powder

½ teaspoon baking soda

½ teaspoon salt

¼ teaspoon dry mustard

⅛ teaspoon cayenne pepper

1 cup coarsely grated sharp Cheddar cheese

2 tablespoons freshly grated Parmesan cheese

¼ cup vegetable oil

1 cup buttermilk

1 large egg

Preheat the oven to 400°F. Grease a muffin tin. Stir the flour, cornmeal, baking powder and soda, salt, mustard, and cayenne together in a large bowl. Toss together with the cheeses. In a small bowl, whisk the oil, buttermilk, and egg together until well blended. Stir the wet ingredients into the dry just until the flour is moistened.

Spoon the batter into the muffin tin and bake until well puffed and golden brown, 18 to 20 minutes. Let sit for 3 minutes, then remove from the tin to cool on a rack for 10 minutes before serving.

COUNTRY TIPS AND TALES

All muffins freeze well for up to 1 month. I pop the cooled muffins into self-sealing plastic bags and then take out only what I need. Let them thaw, then split and toast, or leave them whole, wrap in aluminum foil, and reheat in a preheated 350°F oven.

Brown-Bread Muffins

MAKES 12 MUFFINS

These triple-grain muffins are reminiscent of the hearty steamed breads of earlier days. They make a delicious base for cheeses or can be spread with honey or marmalade. Served with Smoked Ham Hock and Pea Soup (page 110), they make anyone feel like an old-time New Englander.

1 cup whole-wheat flour

⅔ cup rye flour

⅔ cup cornmeal

2 teaspoons baking powder

1 teaspoon baking soda

½ teaspoon salt

¼ cup unsulfured molasses

¼ cup vegetable oil

1 large egg, beaten

1¼ cups buttermilk

½ cup raisins

Preheat the oven to 375°F. Place the flours, cornmeal, baking powder and soda, and salt in a large bowl and stir together. In a small bowl, mix the molasses, oil, egg, and buttermilk until well combined. Stir the wet ingredients into the dry just until the flour is moistened. Stir in the raisins.

Spoon the batter into the muffin tin and bake until browned, 18 to 20 minutes. Let sit 3 minutes, then remove from the tin to cool on a rack for 10 minutes before serving.

COUNTRY TIPS AND TALES

Baking powder was invented in the United States in the 1790s. Before that time leavening agents were salt, eggs, hand-beating to incorporate air into the dough, yeast, and saleratus, or baking soda. A substitute for 1 teaspoon baking powder is ¼ teaspoon baking soda plus ⅝ teaspoon cream of tartar.

Mom's Doughnuts

My mother-in-law makes raised doughnuts that melt in your mouth. All the grandchildren clamor for her to make them, and some have been known not to share. An electric frying pan makes this job easy, otherwise you will need a candy or deep-frying thermometer and a deep pot. She says that all the ingredients should be at room temperature for best results and prefers using Crisco as the shortening. She makes the dough by hand, kneading for 20 minutes, but I use the mixer and get the job done faster. To cover the doughnuts with sugar, we keep an empty Quaker Oats container filled with confectioners' sugar to shake the warm doughnuts in. Doughnuts freeze well in plastic bags when cooled. They will keep for at least 1 month. Then you can pull one out, thaw it, heat it up in the toaster oven, and shake it with sugar.

    6 cups all-purpose flour
    1 tablespoon (1 envelope) dry yeast
    ¼ cup granulated sugar
    ¼ cup (½ stick) unsalted butter
    1½ teaspoons pure vanilla extract
    1 teaspoon salt
    1 cup milk
    1 cup water
    1 large egg
    4 cups vegetable shortening for frying
    Confectioners' sugar

Place all the ingredients, except the shortening and confectioners' sugar, in the bowl of an electric mixer fitted with a dough hook and stir on slow speed until all the ingredients are blended. Continue to knead the dough until smooth and satiny, about 10 minutes. Occasionally scrape down the sides of the bowl. The dough will be very sticky. Sprinkle heavily with flour, cover the bowl with a clean kitchen towel, and let rise in a warm, draft-free place until doubled in volume, about 1½ hours.

continued

Scrape the dough out onto a floured worktable and sprinkle with flour. With a floured rolling pin, roll the dough out ½ inch thick. Cut into circles with a floured doughnut cutter and place the circles on a kitchen towel about 1 inch apart, holes too. Cover with another kitchen towel and let rise for 30 minutes.

Heat the shortening to 370° to 375°F in an electric frying pan or a deep pot fitted with a frying thermometer. Fry several circles of dough at a time. Do not crowd the pan or the temperature will drop, making for greasy doughnuts. Drain on brown paper bags or paper towels. Cool to warm before shaking them with confectioners' sugar. Alternatively, shake the doughnuts in granulated sugar mixed with a bit of cinnamon.

Vegetable Side Dishes and Pickles

AS MUCH AS I enjoy the turkey, it is the trimmings, or side dishes, that really interest me. Vegetables are incredibly versatile. Dress them up or not, just don't cook them to death! The boiled and soggy vegetables that we have all pushed around on our plates have given way to crisp-tender stir-fries, crunchy salads, and colorful appeal. Even the puddings are cooked with a light hand and a very different sensibility.

Years ago, a housewife was really dependent on her garden's productivity in the summer if she were to have enough to serve the family in the wintertime. Storage was limited to cold cellars. Beatrice Vaughan, in "From a Hill-Country Kitchen," remembers, "The house was no less provided for against the months of cold and snow. In the cellar, bins of potatoes, heaps of pumpkins and squashes crowded the barrels of apples and stoneware crocks of good salt pork. On the long shelves where Mother stored her canning, hundreds of glass jars of fruit and vegetables rubbed elbows with those containing beef, pork, and chicken."

Making pickles and sauerkraut provided the family with a source of vitamins as well as with a way to perk up the appetite. Each nationality has its preserved specialty, from Korean kimchi to Jewish kosher dill pickles, condiments that make a supper all the tastier.

My grandmother routinely made open-crock pickled beets and cucumbers at the hotel where we spent all our summers, and I learned about canning from my farm-wife mother-in-law. Her cellar shelves contain jars of stewed tomatoes, tomato juice, pickled cauliflower, beets, dill and sweet pickles, and many varieties of fruits. She still makes jelly from the Concord grapes that grow around her vegetable garden.

Rachel Peden describes in her lovely book *Rural Free: A Farmwife's Almanac of Country Living* a kitchen in full swing during the "canning moon." Her husband was only assured of bread and butter for supper when the moon was in this busy phase. Canning is a big job made a little easier by putting up small batches of pickles or preserves over many days' time. Of course, when the ripe tomatoes start coming in, that is the time. As the old saying goes, "Many hands make the work light," so invite your friends to share in the work and in the bounty.

Now our markets are brimming with produce year-round and we are encouraged to eat unripe, insipid out-of-season vegetables. Better to enjoy these vegetables at the height of their season and put away what we can freeze, dry, or can at that time of peak flavor. I would rather eat canned tomatoes in January than buy those pitiful ones in the store, and anticipate with real delight the coming summer.

Country-Style Greens

MAKES 4 SERVINGS

Greens are easy to grow in our cold climate. They are sown in the early spring and again in August. A mix of mild and spicy greens makes a great salad as well as a cooked vegetable. Tender young greens are best to sauté, needing only the water that clings to them from washing. Vary the greens for interesting flavors. Swiss chard, spinach, bok choy, mustard greens, arugula, dandelion, and chicory are all delicious cooked in this manner. As a variation, try substituting some bacon, cut into ½-inch pieces, for the olive oil and cook until the bacon begins to brown, about 5 minutes, then add the greens.

16 cups mixed tender greens, such as beet greens, spinach, red and green
    Swiss chard, and romaine
1 tablespoon olive oil
1 clove garlic, peeled and minced
¼ teaspoon salt
Freshly ground black pepper to taste

Wash the greens in several changes of water and drain in a colander. Heat the oil in a large skillet over medium heat and cook the garlic for 1 minute. Add the greens, sprinkle with the salt and pepper, and toss. Cook just until wilted, 3 to 4 minutes, and serve. They are also good served at room temperature.

COUNTRY TIPS AND TALES

Sixteen cups of greens may seem like an incredible amount, but greens cook down so much that you need a great deal to end up with a little.

Sweet Corn and Chive Pudding

MAKES 4 TO 6 SERVINGS

My husband is a prodigious eater of sweet corn. As a child growing up on a farm, he remembers his mother putting on a big pot of water to boil and only then going to the garden to pick the corn. His family would easily eat six ears apiece after having eaten their supper! This pudding is actually a soufflé and, if sweetened a little more, could be a dessert.

½ cup milk

½ cup snipped fresh chives

4 cups corn kernels from 6 ears cooked corn, scraped off the cobs with a sharp knife

2 tablespoons all-purpose flour

1 tablespoon sugar

½ teaspoon salt

4 large eggs, separated

1 tablespoon unsalted butter, at room temperature

Preheat the oven to 400°F. Grease an ovenproof 2-quart baking dish. Steep the milk and chives in a medium-size saucepan over low heat for 10 minutes. Puree the corn and hot milk together in a blender or food processor. The mixture will not be smooth. Return the puree to the saucepan and add the flour, sugar, and salt. Cook over medium heat, stirring constantly, until the mixture is boiling. Remove from the heat and let cool, stirring occasionally, for a few minutes. Whisk in the egg yolk, then the butter.

Beat the egg whites with a pinch of salt in a large bowl using an electric mixer on medium speed until soft peaks form. Do not overbeat or the whites will be difficult to fold in. Stir one-quarter of the egg whites into the corn mixture, then gently fold in the rest. Pour into the baking dish and bake until puffed and golden brown, about 30 minutes.

Fresh Corn Fritters

MAKES TWENTY-SIX 3-INCH FRITTERS FOR 4 TO 6 SERVINGS

My brothers-in-law, Omer and Paul, who live in Sharon Springs,
New York, tell of a ham supper near them that serves dough fritters. Maple syrup is the thing to serve over the fritters, they say. While
there are many recipes for corn fritters, these featherlight fritters are
some of the best. I like to serve them with ham or as a supper dish on
their own with sour cream and salsa, even though they do taste great
with syrup.

2 cups fresh corn kernels

2 large eggs

1 cup milk

⅔ cup cornmeal

⅓ cup all-purpose flour

½ teaspoon salt

¼ teaspoon freshly ground black pepper

½ cup canola oil for frying

In a medium-size bowl, combine all ingredients except the oil and stir until well
blended. Heat 3 tablespoons of the oil in a large skillet over medium heat until very

hot. Drop 2 tablespoons for each fritter of the corn batter into the hot oil. Don't crowd the pan; make only 4 or 5 fritters at a time. Cook each fritter until lightly browned, 1 to 2 minutes on each side. Drain on paper towels and cover loosely with a sheet of aluminum foil to keep warm, while cooking the remaining batter. Add more oil to the skillet as needed.

Kohlrabi Salad with Mary's Prize Dressing

MAKES 4 TO 6 SERVINGS

Mary Jirik hails from Minnesota and with her husband, Mort Brown, a seventh-generation Vermonter, runs an organic farm. Mary cans and sells jams and pickles at the farmers' market in Rutland. Last year at the Barre Farm Show, she won a ribbon for this dressing, which combines beautifully with shredded kohlrabi. Kohlrabi, that funny-looking vegetable, comes in green or purple varieties and is sweet and crunchy with a mild cabbage flavor.

This dish is a refreshing winter salad that will perk up tired palates.

¼ cup pure dark amber or grade B maple syrup

½ teaspoon salt

3 tablespoons cider vinegar

½ cup canola oil

¾ teaspoon dry mustard

1 teaspoon poppy seeds

1 pound kohlrabi, peeled and coarsely shredded

3 navel oranges

Romaine lettuce leaves

Mix the maple syrup, salt, vinegar, oil, mustard, and poppy seeds together in a large bowl and whisk until well blended. Toss with the kohlrabi. Cut off all the peel and white pith from the oranges and cut them into sections. Add the orange sections to the kohlrabi and toss. Line a serving bowl with romaine lettuce leaves and spoon the kohlrabi into the center.

Apple, Chestnut, and Chayote Salad

MAKES 4 TO 6 SERVINGS

Fresh chestnuts are only available in the fall around the very busy holiday season, so when I discovered canned whole chestnuts, I was grateful not to have to roast and peel them myself. These work well, as do dried chestnuts (page 3), which are available in Chinese and Italian groceries and in some health food stores.

Chayote is a pale green, pear-shaped squash, also known as "cristophine" or "mirliton," that is sweet and crunchy when served raw in salads. This combination makes a crisp accompaniment to a winter supper of Macaroni and Chicken in Cheddar Sauce (page 49).

    2 medium-size tart apples, such as Granny Smith, unpeeled, cored, and diced
    1 cup crumbled chestnuts
    1 cup peeled and diced chayote squash
    2 tablespoons fresh lemon juice
    ¾ teaspoon salt
    ¼ teaspoon freshly ground black pepper
    ⅓ cup pure olive oil
    1 tablespoon finely chopped fresh chervil or parsley leaves
    6 romaine lettuce leaves

Place the apples, chestnuts, and chayote in a medium-size nonreactive bowl. Whisk the lemon juice, salt, and pepper together in a small bowl, then whisk in the olive oil until well blended. Stir in the chervil. Pour over the apple mixture and toss to coat. Let the salad sit for 1 hour at room temperature to allow the flavors to develop, then adjust the seasoning. Place a romaine leaf on each salad plate and spoon the salad on top.

Red and Green Cabbage Salad

Many community suppers include very tasty coleslaws, but I grew tired of the mayonnaise-based salads and so developed this colorful and piquant challenger, which has become a staple in our house.

4 cups finely shredded green cabbage

2 cups finely shredded red cabbage

½ cup slivered red onions

¼ cup cider vinegar

1 tablespoon grainy prepared mustard

½ teaspoon salt

¼ teaspoon freshly ground black pepper

1 tablespoon chopped fresh dill or 1 teaspoon dried

¼ cup canola oil

Place the cabbages and onions in a large nonreactive bowl. Place the vinegar, mustard, salt, pepper, and dill in a small bowl and whisk together. Whisk in the oil until well combined and pour over the cabbage, tossing to coat. Let the salad sit for 2 hours at room temperature to allow the flavors to develop, tossing occasionally, before serving.

COUNTRY TIPS AND TALES

Known as "colewart" in folk medicine and used since 400 B.C., cabbage is said to be beneficial for healing stomach ulcers, for a joint tonic, and for skin problems and fevers.

Shrewsbury Potato Salad

MAKES 6 TO 8 SERVINGS

Many people in the town of Shrewsbury contribute their special salads to the Firemen's Supper held in early autumn each year. Mary Reed often contributed her apple pies and potato salad, and you were lucky if you got to sit at the table where her salad was served.

2 pounds boiling potatoes, peeled and cut into 1-inch chunks
1½ teaspoons salt
1 cup diced onions
1 cup seeded and diced green bell peppers
4 hard-boiled eggs, peeled
½ cup mayonnaise
2 tablespoons vegetable oil
¼ teaspoon freshly ground black pepper
Sweet Hungarian paprika

Place the potatoes in a 3-quart saucepan and cover with cold water. Add 1 teaspoon of the salt and bring to a boil over medium heat. Reduce the heat to medium-low and cook until the potatoes are tender when pierced with a fork, about 15 minutes. Drain and place in a large bowl with the onions and peppers. Coarsely chop the eggs and add them to the bowl. Stir in the mayonnaise, oil, the remaining ½ teaspoon salt, and the pepper and mix very well. Sprinkle the surface with paprika. Cover with plastic wrap and refrigerate until ready to serve.

COUNTRY TIPS AND TALES

Always plant potatoes in the dark of the moon.
—An old country saying

Scalloped Potatoes

Dishes of creamy potatoes often show up at community suppers featuring ham. I have seen the most ardent dieters buckle when presented with a plate of these golden potatoes. You can also make them into a main dish by adding leftover ham or smoked haddock.

    1 tablespoon unsalted butter
    3 pounds boiling potatoes, unpeeled
    Salt and freshly ground black pepper to taste
    2 cups heavy cream

Preheat the oven to 350°F. Butter an ovenproof 2-quart baking dish or a 9 × 13-inch baking dish with half the butter. Slice the potatoes very thinly and cook for 4 minutes in a large pot of boiling salted water over high heat. Drain in a colander. Place one third of the potatoes in the baking dish, sprinkle with salt and pepper, and drizzle with some of the cream. Repeat two more times, using up all of the cream. Dot the top with the remaining butter. Bake, uncovered, until the top is golden brown and the potatoes are tender when pierced with a fork, about 1 hour.

COUNTRY TIPS AND TALES

One of Murphy's Laws is that every time you make scalloped potatoes, they spill over on the oven floor and make a mess. Of course, the smart cook puts the baking dish on a cookie sheet to catch any spills.

Garden Colcannon

MAKES 4 TO 6 SERVINGS

Found in Irish and Scottish cookbooks, colcannon is a savory mash of potatoes and green onions. Some cooks prepare this dish with cabbage, some with carrots or turnips. This colcannon combines the products of my garden—tall, sweet leeks and my favorite root vegetable, parsnips, with potato.

3 large boiling potatoes, peeled and cubed
2 large parsnips, peeled, cored, and cubed
3 tablespoons unsalted butter
2 large leeks, white and pale green parts only, thoroughly washed
    and thinly sliced
Salt and freshly ground black pepper to taste

Cook the potatoes and parsnips in a large pot of boiling salted water until tender, 20 to 25 minutes. Drain, reserving ½ cup of the cooking liquid. Mash the vegetables with the reserved liquid and set aside.

Heat the butter in a large skillet and cook the leeks, stirring, over medium heat until lightly browned, about 15 minutes. Add the mashed vegetables and season to taste. Stir until heated through and serve.

COUNTRY TIPS AND TALES

An old custom of fortune-telling in Nova Scotia
was to serve a dish of "Kohl Cannon" on Halloween.
A penny, a match, a ring, and a button would be buried in
the dish and whoever got the hidden prize was said to have
his or her fortune told for the coming year.

Three-Root Mash

Carrots and parsnips are joined by the Swede, or rutabaga, to make this flavorful side dish. Roasting rather than boiling makes this homespun trio triple sweet.

1½ tablespoons pure olive oil

1 pound carrots, quartered

1 pound parsnips, peeled, cored, and quartered

1 pound rutabaga, peeled and cut into ½-inch cubes

½ teaspoon salt

¼ teaspoon freshly ground black pepper

Preheat the oven to 400°F. Oil a baking pan with ½ tablespoon of the oil and spread the vegetables on the pan. Cover the pan tightly with a sheet of aluminum foil and cook until the vegetables are tender when pierced with a fork, about 40 minutes. Mash together with a fork or potato masher, seasoning with salt, pepper, and the remaining tablespoon olive oil. The mixture should be roughly mashed, not pureed. Reheat the mixture briefly in a skillet, stirring, over medium-low heat.

COUNTRY TIPS AND TALES

Overwinter root vegetables by storing them in crates of barely moist sand in a cool, dark cellar.

Rutabaga Gratin

Underneath that unlovely exterior lies a sweet-fleshed yellow turnip called a Swede or rutabaga. Proctor, Vermont, was the center of the marble industry, which brought in many immigrant groups to work the quarries. Many Swedish workers settled here and continued to cook their beloved rutabaga.

Most people think they hate rutabaga because it has been boiled to death by too many indifferent cooks. Perhaps this recipe will change their minds.

2 tablespoons unsalted butter

1 large rutabaga, peeled and coarsely grated (about 6 cups)

2 shallots, finely chopped

1 tablespoon firmly packed light brown sugar

½ teaspoon salt

¼ teaspoon freshly ground black pepper

½ cup shredded Swiss or Gruyère cheese

2 tablespoons dried bread crumbs

Preheat the oven to 400°F. Grease a 9½-inch deep pie plate or a 1-quart gratin dish. Heat the butter in a large skillet over medium heat and stir in the rutabaga and shallots. Add the sugar, salt, and pepper and cook, stirring occasionally, until the rutabaga is tender, about 30 minutes. Spoon into the pie plate or gratin dish and sprinkle with the cheese and bread crumbs. Bake until the cheese is melted and browned, about 20 minutes. Serve hot.

COUNTRY TIPS AND TALES

Anyone who grew up in New England has to have a dish of mashed rutabagas on the Thanksgiving table.

Cider-Glazed Carrots

MAKES 4 SERVINGS

Boiled cider is a syrup made by cooking down gallons of apple cider. Thus preserved, the syrup could be reconstituted with water throughout the year. It also makes a delicious drizzle on vanilla ice cream and this tangy carrot dish. Willis and Tina Woods make the syrupy cider in Springfield and will send you more good recipes for its use (see Mail-Order Sources, page 255).

1½ pounds carrots, cut into ½-inch-thick slices on the diagonal
1 tablespoon unsalted butter
½ teaspoon salt
½ cup water
2 tablespoons boiled cider
1 tablespoon cider vinegar

Place the carrots, butter, salt, and water in a medium-size nonreactive saucepan with a tightly fitting cover. Bring to a boil over medium heat, reduce the heat to medium-low, and cook for about 10 minutes. Uncover and add the cider and vinegar. Raise the heat to high and, swirling the pan to prevent sticking, let the liquid reduce to a glaze that just coats the carrots, about 15 minutes. Serve hot.

COUNTRY TIPS AND TALES

Celia Murphy remembers how she ate cider jelly as a child. Her mother boiled down the cider into a thick, jelly-like mass, then added sliced sweet apples. She put the mixture in a barrel and kept it in a very cold room. During the severe winter months, she would chop off a piece, thaw it out, and serve it as dessert.

Little Maple-Baked Squashes

MAKES 8 SERVINGS

When the squash is sweet, one could eat this dish for dessert. Indeed, this simple preparation is the forerunner of puddings and pies utilizing this indigenous vegetable. Use any little squashes or pumpkins just big enough for one serving. I find the little sweet dumplings, small acorn squashes, or mini-pumpkins make festive presentations for the holidays. Simple as these are, you can use your creativity to think of more stuffings.

8 small Sweet Dumpling squashes

8 teaspoons unsalted butter

1 cup pure dark amber or grade B maple syrup

Salt and freshly ground black pepper to taste

Ground cinnamon to taste

Preheat the oven to 400°F. Cut a lid from each squash about 1 inch from the stem. Scoop out the seeds with a grapefruit knife or a spoon. Place the squashes close together in a baking pan and pour in ½ inch of water. Place 1 teaspoon of the butter and 2 tablespoons of the syrup in each squash and sprinkle each with the salt and pepper and cinnamon. Replace the lids. Tightly cover the dish with a sheet of aluminum foil and bake until the squashes are tender when pierced with a fork, about 40 minutes. Lift the squashes carefully onto a serving platter.

COUNTRY TIPS AND TALES

Squash is one of the "three sisters," along with corn and pole beans, that were the mainstay of Native American diets.

Dilled Peas and Mushrooms

MAKES 4 TO 6 SERVINGS

The vegetables were the best part of this church supper in Newfane. At the table, we chatted with an elderly woman, who had grown up in the town and witnessed many changes. Later, we strolled around town, with its stately matching white-and-green-shuttered church, meeting house, and court house, trying to envision an earlier time.

Here is an instance where the convenience of a frozen product matches the quality of fresh. Frozen baby or petite peas are terrific and you can forget the shelling.

2 tablespoons unsalted butter

½ cup finely chopped onions

2 cups sliced mushrooms

½ teaspoon salt

¼ teaspoon freshly ground black pepper

One 1-pound package or two 10-ounce packages frozen petite peas, thawed

2 tablespoons chopped fresh dill

Heat the butter in a large skillet over medium heat and cook the onions, stirring, until softened, about 5 minutes. Add the mushrooms, salt, and pepper and cook, stirring occasionally, until the mushrooms are softened and juicy, 6 to 7 minutes. Stir in the peas and dill and cook just until the peas are heated through.

COUNTRY TIPS AND TALES

Frozen peas have been blanched before freezing and don't need much more cooking than reheating; this way they will keep their lovely bright color.

Roasted Beets in Honey-Orange Dressing

I am quite fond of beets and look for interesting ways to serve them. Roasting beets makes them intensely sweet, and even those people who often look askance at beets will change their view having tried them. Reserve the greens for Country-Style Greens (page 133). This dish goes well on a summer supper buffet. This may be made 1 to 2 days ahead and refrigerated, but bring to room temperature before serving for full flavor.

> 2 pounds 2-inch beets, greens removed, leaving an inch of stem
> ¼ cup orange juice
> 2 tablespoons fresh lemon juice
> 1 tablespoon honey
> 1 tablespoon grainy prepared mustard
> ¼ teaspoon salt
> Freshly ground black pepper to taste
> 2 tablespoons olive oil

Preheat the oven to 400°F. Scrub the beets thoroughly and wrap them up tightly in aluminum foil. Roast on the center rack of the oven until you can pierce the beets through with a fork, about 1 hour. Remove from the oven, unwrap the beets, and let cool until they can be handled. The skins should be easy to remove if you scrape them with a sharp knife. Cut the beets into cubes.

Whisk the orange and lemon juices, honey, mustard, salt, and pepper together in a bowl. Whisk in the oil. Toss the beets with the dressing. Let stand at room temperature for an hour before serving so the flavors can blend.

Chris and Andy's Maple-Pickled Beets

MAKES 10 PINTS

Chris Anderson and Andy Snyder run Fire Hill Farm in Florence, Vermont. They sell their organically grown foods through the mail and at their Weston farm stand. Using their maple syrup to sweeten jams and pickles gives all of these products a mellow flavor. I catered their wedding one hot July day sixteen years ago, on the farm up in the hills full of wild flowers.

10 pounds 1-inch beets, thoroughly washed

8½ cups cider vinegar

4 cups pure dark amber or grade B maple syrup

3 cups water

1⅓ tablespoons canning salt

1⅓ tablespoons allspice berries

1 cinnamon stick

Sterilize the jars and lids by placing them in a deep soup or canning kettle with a rack in the bottom. Cover with water and bring to a boil. Let sit in the water off the heat while you prepare the beets.

Trim the greens from the beets, leaving 1 inch; reserve the greens for another use. Cook the beets in a large pot of boiling water until the skins slip off easily, 25 to 30 minutes. Drain, and when cool enough to handle, skin the beets, removing the stems. Drain the jars and lids on a clean kitchen towel. Cut the beets into ¼-inch-thick slices and pack into the sterilized pint jars.

Place the vinegar, maple syrup, water, canning salt, allspice, and cinnamon stick in a large nonreactive pot and bring to a boil over medium heat. Reduce the heat to medium-low and cook for 10 minutes. Discard the cinnamon stick and pour the liquid over the beets, leaving ½ inch of head space. Be sure to put a few allspice berries into each jar. Run a knife around the insides of each jar to release any air bubbles. Wipe the rims clean and seal the jars.

Place the jars on a rack in a large pot of boiling water. The water should come 2 inches above the canning jars. Tightly cover the pot when the water is boiling and boil for 20 minutes. Remove the jars and cool them on a kitchen towel. If properly sealed, the jars will ping as they cool down and the lids become concave. Cool 12 hours and check the seals. Store any jars in the refrigerator that did not seal and eat these beets first. Store the other jars in a cool, dark place. Refrigerate after opening.

Cranberry Apple Chutney

MAKES 1½ QUARTS

Easily made, this chutney keeps well in a covered container in the refrigerator for months. I like to make it several weeks before it is needed to allow the flavors time to develop. It is a great accompaniment to a ham, roast pork, or turkey supper and even goes well with chicken pot pie.

One 12-ounce package fresh cranberries
2 pounds tart apples, such as greening or Granny Smith, cored, peeled, and
    cut into chunks
Juice and grated zest of 1 orange
1 cup golden raisins
1 large clove garlic, peeled
1 small dried or fresh hot pepper or ½ teaspoon crushed red pepper
One 1-inch piece fresh ginger
1 cup cider vinegar
½ cup firmly packed light brown sugar
1 cinnamon stick
1 teaspoon cumin seeds
1 teaspoon salt
½ teaspoon coriander seeds
½ teaspoon mustard seeds
6 whole cloves

continued

Place all the ingredients in a large nonreactive saucepan and bring to a boil over medium heat, stirring occasionally. Reduce the heat to low and cook until very thick, about 1 hour. Stir occasionally to prevent the chutney from sticking to the pan. Spoon into a nonreactive container, cover, and refrigerate for at least 3 weeks before serving.

COUNTRY TIPS AND TALES

Nose, nose, jolly red nose
And who gave thee this jolly red nose? . . .
Nutmegs and ginger, cinnamon and cloves,
And they gave me this jolly red nose.
—Francis Beaumont (1584—1616), *The Knight of the Burning Pestle*

Bread and Butter Summer Squash Pickles

MAKES 6 PINT JARS

When the zucchini and the yellow squash have overstayed their welcome, make pickles from them. On a dreary winter evening, a jar of squash pickles will remind you that summer surely will return. These sweet-and-sour pickles can be made with all zucchini or a combination of yellow and green summer squash.

4 pounds summer squash, cut into ¼-inch-thick slices
1 pound onions, peeled and sliced
¼ cup plus 1½ teaspoons canning salt
1 quart crushed ice
2¼ cups cider vinegar

1 cup pure dark amber or grade B maple syrup

¾ cup water

1 tablespoon mustard seeds

1 teaspoon allspice berries

1 teaspoon turmeric

½ teaspoon celery seeds

⅛ teaspoon cayenne pepper

Place the squash and onions in a large bowl and toss with the ¼ cup of salt and the ice. Cover the vegetables with a plate and place a 5-pound weight on the plate. Let sit for 3 to 4 hours.

Sterilize the jars and lids by placing them in a deep soup or canning kettle with a rack in the bottom. Cover with water and bring to a boil. Let sit in the water off the heat until needed.

Drain the vegetables in a colander. Combine the vegetables in a large nonreactive pot with the remaining 1½ teaspoons salt, the vinegar, maple syrup, water, and spices. Bring to a boil over high heat.

Drain the jars and lids on a clean kitchen towel. Pack the vegetables into the sterilized jars and pour in the liquid, leaving ¼ inch of head space. Run a knife around the insides of each jar to release any air bubbles. Wipe the rims clean and seal the jars. Place the jars on a rack in a large pot of boiling water. The water should come 2 inches above the jars. Tightly cover the pot and process for 20 minutes. Remove the jars and cool them on kitchen towels. If properly sealed, the jars will ping as they cool down and the lids become concave. Cool 12 hours and check the seals. Store any jars in the refrigerator that did not seal and eat these pickles first. Store the others in a cool, dark place. Refrigerate after opening.

COUNTRY TIPS AND TALES

An entry in an 1874 diary reads: "Oct. 6—Been getting up sweet corn to dry this afternoon. All went out and picked up potatoes with Albro. Mary stayed in to make sweet pickles."
—*Green Mountain Whittlin's*

Great-Grandma Hoff's
Sour Crock Pickles

MAKES 10 POUNDS PICKLES

Hailing from Pennsylvania Dutch stock and raised in Ohio, Trish Norton passed on this recipe from her great-grandmother. Trish's little girls are fifth-generation pickle nibblers and they love to snack on these crunchy sour treats. This open-crock method allows for quick pickling, and as Trish's garden is bountiful, she continues to toss in some green beans and small green tomatoes as well as small cucumbers. These pickles will last up to 3 to 4 months, providing no one gobbles them up sooner.

Grape leaves are traditionally used to help keep open-crock pickles crisp. They grow wild all around here.

10 pounds small cucumbers (3 inches long is ideal), washed
1 gallon cider vinegar
1 cup canning salt
1 cup dry mustard
1 cup grated horseradish
1 cup pure dark amber or grade B maple syrup
1 or 2 fresh grape leaves, washed

Clean and scald a 3-gallon crock or a heavy-duty plastic pail. Place the cucumbers in the crock. Stir the vinegar, salt, mustard, horseradish, and maple syrup together in a large bowl and pour over the cucumbers. Place the grape leaves on the top and cover with a plate weighted down with a clean 5-pound stone. Place a kitchen towel over the top and store in a cool, dark place. The pickles will be ready to eat in 3 days when their color turns yellowish.

We store these pickles in the cellar where the temperature remains above freezing. So does Trish. If you haven't a cellar, a cool garage will do, if it remains above freezing. Just leave them in the crock.

Sweet-and-Sour Carrots, Cauliflower, and Peppers

MAKES 12 CUPS

Make this easy pickle and keep it in the refrigerator for up to a year! The vegetables stay crisp and crunchy all that time and very colorful. If you really like hot pickles, find a whole habanero chile pepper to use. But beware! This little drum-shaped pepper (also called Scotch bonnet) is one of the hottest chiles in existence.

3 quarts water
1 large cauliflower, cut into florets
3 large green bell peppers, seeded and cut into strips
3 large red bell peppers, seeded and cut into strips
1 pound carrots, cut into thin sticks
2 small fresh hot peppers
3 cups sugar
3 cups white vinegar
1½ teaspoons salt
1½ cups water

Bring the water to a boil over high heat and add the vegetables. Immediately turn off the heat and let the vegetables sit for 2 minutes. Drain the vegetables in a colander and spread them out on a kitchen towel to dry. When cool, pack them in sterilized glass containers.

Mix the sugar, vinegar, salt, and water together in a large nonreactive saucepan and bring to a boil over medium heat. Stir occasionally to dissolve the sugar. Cool the pickling liquid and pour over the vegetables. Tightly cover the containers and store in the refrigerator. Let the pickles sit at least 1 week before serving to allow the flavors to develop.

Hot Basil Beans

MAKES 4 PINT JARS

Chris Anderson and Andy Snyder of Fire Hill Farm in Florence have given dilly beans a new twist by using basil. You can add as many hot peppers as your taste dictates. Our son, Simon, gets care packages of these pickled beans now that he is living far from Vermont. Try to use beans that are similar in size for the most attractive results.

> 2 pounds green beans, trimmed
> 4 small fresh hot peppers (if using habanero,
>   add only ¼ of 1 pepper to each jar)
> 4 cloves garlic, peeled
> 4 fresh sprigs basil
> 2½ cups water
> 2½ cups cider vinegar
> ¼ cup canning salt

Sterilize the jars and lids by placing them in a deep soup or canning kettle with a rack in the bottom. Cover with water and bring to a boil. Let sit in the water off the heat while you prepare the beans.

Drain the jars and lids on a clean kitchen towel. Pack the beans into the sterilized jars. Add a hot pepper, garlic clove, and basil sprig to each jar. Place the water, vinegar, and salt in a large nonreactive saucepan and bring to a boil over medium heat. Pour the boiling liquid over the beans, leaving ¼ inch head space at the top. Run a knife around the insides of each jar to release any air bubbles. Wipe the rims clean and seal the jars. Place the jars on a rack in a large pot of boiling water. Process for 20 minutes. Remove the jars and cool them on kitchen towels. If properly sealed, the jars will ping as they cool down and the lids become concave. Cool for 12 hours and check the seals.

Store any jars in the refrigerator that did not seal and eat these beans first. Let the beans sit in a cool, dark place for at least 2 weeks before serving to allow the flavors to develop. Refrigerate after opening.

COUNTRY TIPS AND TALES

Never, ever process a low-acid vegetable in a water bath unless it is in a vinegar brine to prevent the growth of bacteria that cause botulism, a potentially fatal disease. Read the *Ball Blue Book* (see Bibliography) to answer all your canning questions; it is an indispensable tool for the home canner.

Fruit Desserts and Preserves

"**E**VERYBODY WENT TO THE party where amid wagging tongues and bursts of laughter, the work of paring and quartering apples went on. Soon as the last basket was reached and disposed of, and pans and peelings gathered up, the party started." Get-togethers like this one recalled in Volume 6 of *Green Mountain Whittlin's* were common types of kitchen parties, or "tunks." (A tunk might be a thump, which heavy boots would have made on wooden floors after the rug was rolled up; or tunk might be a corruption of dunk, when dunking for apples was a kitchen party pastime.)

Vermont is well known for apples and apple products, like apple cider, boiled cider, and cider jelly. On a crisp, glorious day in the fall, nothing beats a drive through our woods and a drink of freshly pressed, fragrant cider. After the first frost, I love to bite into a crisp MacIntosh apple, sweet and tangy, the juice dripping down my chin.

Some old apple varieties are returning and farmers are planting these new-old apples with lovely names like Pound Sweet, Duchess of Oldenburg, and Westfield Seek-No-Further. Many pear varieties, like many apple varieties, have been bred out of existence. An 1898 cookbook mentions pears such as English Jargonelle, Windsor, and Green Chisel. The French have a variety called Cuisse de Dames, or ladies' thighs. Trust the French to recognize the sensual connection between food and sex!

Early harvested apples make good pies, but the later ones keep better. Drying apples was a common way to store the harvest and many recipes were invented by creative cooks to use the dehydrated apples, such as fried, dried apple pies. Throughout this book, apples in their many forms, from fresh to sauce, are combined with other foods to sweeten and flavor many dishes.

Any recipe made with apples can be made with pears. Most pears grown in Vermont come from the more southern sections of the state. Usually only the hardy little Seckels can survive our harsh winters, but sometimes a gardener is lucky and has a pear tree that doesn't seem to mind where it lives and flourishes.

The flavors of each variety of pear are quite different. The winey flavor of the Anjou pear, the sweetness of the Bartlett, the firm, buttery taste of the Bosc make eating and cooking with pears a delight. One of the most memorable food experiences of my life involved a pear: the most perfect pear, silky in texture, an aroma like perfume, eaten with a slice of Gorgonzola, while sitting on a bench in the golden ocher sunset of Pisa, Italy. It was better than a three-star meal.

Pears continue to have my affection, for once when I was both pregnant and with flu, my mother-in-law fed me her sweet home-canned pears and I felt better. Pears can be like royalty, as in that famous dish Poires Belle Hélène, or homey like Mary's Brown-Sugar Seckels (page 205). And probably I love pears because they are shaped just like me!

Berries have always been special. Perhaps it is because the ripe fruit is hidden away behind leaves and sometimes thorns or perhaps because the birds will clean out your berries if you don't cover the bushes with netting. Perhaps it is because berries are the essence of summer.

Strawberry socials celebrate the harvest at the end of June with suppers culminating in strawberry desserts. We took a trip over to Westminster along the wide Connecticut River to partake of a fine ham supper that ended with huge bowls of strawberry shortcake. There was quite a line and a long wait, for word gets around when a community supper is a good one.

There are a number of nearby farms growing strawberries and it is really enjoyable to spend a few hours in the sun picking berries. Children love squatting on the straw mulch, getting their mouths and fingers stained with red juice. We try to pick enough berries to eat fresh, to freeze for winter, and to make jam. That's about twenty quarts of berries.

One disappointing cold and rainy June yielded too few berries for the annual Clarendon Brick Church's Strawberry Social and we had to make do with commercially frozen berries. There is no duplicating the aroma and flavor of just-picked sun-ripened strawberries.

Blueberry bushes growing behind our house yield buckets of big berries, and I simply fill plastic bags and freeze them. Then it is easy to pull out just enough for pancakes or pies all winter long. My mother makes a wonderful blueberry pie that has been the butt of a few family jokes. Twice she had made pies to bring to friends, and twice they slid off the back seat of the car and flopped over. Of course it was my dad's fault for driving so fast!

All through the woods and hillsides grow wild blackberries. In a good year, with enough sun and rain, the berries will be thimble-sized and juicy. Luckily, we get to the berries before the bears or birds and pick our fill. We make sure to wear long sleeves and pants, even though the day may be hot, because blackberry bushes, known as bramble bushes, are very thorny.

Baked Maple Apples

MAKES 6 SERVINGS

The McWaters family have one of those old trees in their backyard in Blissville that produces apples larger than grapefruit, called Pound Sweets. I was really amazed the first time I saw them. One apple is big enough for a pie! For baked apples, though, you need a small apple that will hold its shape during baking, like a Northern Spy or Cortland.

6 large apples
3 tablespoons unsalted butter, melted
⅔ cup fresh whole-wheat bread crumbs
⅔ cup pure dark amber or grade B maple syrup
Heavy cream (optional)

Preheat the oven to 350°F. Remove a 1-inch-wide strip of peel from the stem end of each apple with a swivel-bladed peeler. Core the apples and place them in a 9-inch cake pan or a baking pan small enough to pack the apples closely together.

Mix the butter with the bread crumbs in a small bowl and stir in 2 tablespoons of the maple syrup. Place some of this stuffing in the hollowed-out core of each apple. Put ¼ inch of water in the pan and drizzle the remaining syrup over the apples. Cover the pan tightly with a sheet of aluminum foil and bake for 40 minutes. Uncover and spoon some of the juices over the apples. Bake, uncovered, until the apples are tender when pierced with a fork, about 30 minutes more. Serve with the juices from the pan and a pitcher of heavy cream on the side.

COUNTRY TIPS AND TALES

Combinations of fruit and bread can be seen in many old desserts, from charlottes to betties, and stemmed from the school of "waste not, want not."

Apple Oatmeal Crisp

Rustic warm desserts like this one are satisfying to make and lovely to eat. Crisp or crumble toppings can be made ahead and refrigerated in a covered container. This makes it really fast to whip together a dessert on short notice. Whether you need this dish in a hurry or not, it is a good example of hearty country cooking, best accompanied by cream or vanilla ice cream. Of course, you can substitute any fruit for the apples and still be happy. But do not use the quick-cooking type of oats.

2 pounds apples, such as Cortland, McIntosh, or Northern Spy, cored, peeled, and cut into chunks

½ cup dark or golden raisins

⅓ cup granulated sugar

Juice and grated zest of 1 lemon

¾ cup all-purpose flour

⅔ cup old-fashioned rolled oats

¾ cup firmly packed dark brown sugar

⅓ cup unsalted butter, at room temperature

Preheat the oven to 350°F. Grease a 9-inch-square baking pan. Place the apples in the pan and toss them with the raisins, granulated sugar, and lemon juice until evenly coated. Place the grated zest, flour, oats, and brown sugar in a small bowl and rub in the butter with your fingers until thoroughly blended. The mixture will be lumpy.

Sprinkle the flour mixture evenly over the apples and bake until the apples are tender when pierced with a fork and the topping is browned, about 1 hour. Serve warm.

Steamed Apple-Butter Pudding

Vermont harvests millions of apples each year and some of them are made into apple butter—apples cooked very slowly with spices until thick (see page 206 for a recipe). Jars of this sweet spread can be used to make pies and this hot dessert, a satisfying way to end a meal on a cold winter evening.

Fragrant steamed puddings were common fare to the early New Englanders but they have long gone out of fashion. They really can be quite delicious and should be reintroduced to the cooking repertoire. This can be served with Custard Sauce (page 244) or lightly sweetened whipped cream.

½ cup (1 stick) unsalted butter, at room temperature
½ cup firmly packed light brown sugar
⅛ teaspoon salt
3 large eggs
¾ cup apple butter
1 teaspoon baking soda dissolved in 2 tablespoons apple cider
1⅓ cups fresh whole-wheat bread crumbs

Grease well a 6-cup pudding mold or deep bowl. (If your mold is fluted at the top, line it with a ring of parchment or waxed paper to prevent sticking.) In a large bowl, cream the butter, sugar, and salt together with an electric mixer on high speed until light and fluffy. Beat in the eggs, one at a time, scraping down the sides of the bowl after each addition. Stir in the apple butter, baking soda and cider, and bread crumbs until well blended. Scrape the mixture into the mold or deep bowl.

Cover the mold with a sheet of aluminum foil and tie it tightly with kitchen string. (If the mold has a cover, skip this step.) Place the bowl on a rack in a deep saucepan or steamer. Add 3 inches of boiling water, cover, and steam for 2 hours over medium-low heat, adding more boiling water if needed. The pudding is done when the surface looks dry and the texture is firm.

Remove the mold from the steamer and remove the foil. Run a knife around the inside edge to loosen the pudding and invert onto a serving plate. Serve hot, warm, or cold with cream or custard sauce.

Applesauce Walnut Bars

MAKES 16 COOKIES

Last summer was very dry and so were the apples that I gleaned from our neglected, old trees. The applesauce came out tasty but very thick, perfect for these moist bar cookies. If you use a thin commercial applesauce, drain it in a sieve for 15 minutes, and it will be just right. And do not use the quick-cooking type of oats.

1½ cups all-purpose flour

1 cup old-fashioned rolled oats

½ cup chopped walnuts

¾ cup firmly packed light brown sugar

¾ teaspoon baking powder

½ teaspoon salt

½ teaspoon ground cinnamon

½ teaspoon freshly grated nutmeg

½ cup (1 stick) unsalted butter, at room temperature

2 cups thick applesauce

continued

Preheat the oven to 350°F. Grease an 8-inch-square baking pan. Place the flour, oats, walnuts, sugar, baking powder, salt, cinnamon, and nutmeg in a medium-size bowl and rub in the butter with your fingers until thoroughly blended. The mixture will be lumpy.

Firmly press half the mixture into the pan and evenly spread the applesauce on top. Sprinkle the remaining flour mixture evenly over the applesauce and gently press into a smooth layer. Bake on the center rack of the oven until golden brown, 45 to 50 minutes. Cool completely in the pan before cutting into squares.

COUNTRY TIPS AND TALES

Apple varieties have been manipulated for centuries through grafting, to improve keeping ability, to resist diseases, and improve flavor, originally in medieval monasteries by the monks who cultivated the orchards.

"Their syrup is a good cordial in faintings, palpitations, and melancholy."
—Nicholas Culpeper in *The Complete Herbal* (1653)

Chunky Apple Cake

This is *the* cake to bring to suppers. Its unusual texture and great taste will have people asking for the recipe. Make it in a 10-inch bundt pan and you can serve sixteen easily. Try substituting dried cranberries for the golden raisins, chunks of pears for the apples, and pecans for the walnuts. You cannot miss!

3 cups (6 sticks) unsalted butter, melted

4 cups firmly packed light brown sugar

6 large eggs

2 teaspoons pure vanilla extract

6 cups all-purpose flour

1 teaspoon salt

2 teaspoons ground cinnamon

2 teaspoons baking soda

6 cups apples, such as Cortland or Northern Spy, cored, peeled, and cut into 1-inch chunks

2 cups coarsely chopped walnuts

2 cups golden raisins

Confectioners' sugar

Preheat the oven to 350°F. Grease and flour a 10-inch bundt pan, tapping off any excess flour. In a large bowl, beat the butter, brown sugar, eggs, and vanilla together with an electric mixer on high speed until very thick and creamy. Stir together the flour, salt, cinnamon, and baking soda in another large bowl and add gradually, on low speed, to the butter mixture just until the flour is blended. Stir in the apples, nuts, and raisins. The mixture will be very thick.

Scrape the batter into the pan and bake on the center rack of the oven until a toothpick inserted into the center of the cake comes out clean, about 1¼ hours. Cool completely in the pan on a rack. Loosen the edges of the cake with a knife and invert onto a serving plate. The cake needs nothing more than a sprinkle of confectioners' sugar before serving.

Apple Upside-down Cake

MAKES 4 TO 6 SERVINGS

The jeweled look of the glistening fruits is what makes upside-down cakes so pretty and appetizing. Almost any type of fruit can be substituted for the apples. In my last book, *Tomato Imperative!*, I made one using green tomatoes. Try substituting maple sugar for the brown sugar and the light spice cake will have an even better taste.

¼ cup (½ stick) unsalted butter, at room temperature
⅔ cup firmly packed light brown sugar
2 large apples, such as Cortland or Northern Spy, cored, peeled, and thinly
  sliced
3 large eggs, at room temperature
¾ cup all-purpose flour
¾ teaspoon baking powder
½ teaspoon ground cinnamon
¼ teaspoon freshly grated nutmeg
¼ teaspoon salt

Preheat the oven to 350°F. Using 2 tablespoons of the butter, thickly smear the bottom and sides of a 9 × 2-inch round cake pan. Place the remaining 2 tablespoons butter in a small saucepan and melt over low heat. Sprinkle ⅓ cup of the brown sugar over the butter in the pan and press lightly to evenly coat with the sugar. Arrange the apple slices in slightly overlapping circles on top of the brown sugar.

Place the eggs in a medium-size bowl and beat on medium speed with an electric mixer until foamy. Increase the speed to high and beat in the remaining ⅓ cup brown sugar by tablespoons. Beat until the mixture is very thick and drip slowly when the beater is lifted, about 5 minutes. In a small bowl, mix the flour, baking powder, cinnamon, nutmeg, and salt together. At the lowest mixer speed, gradually stir the flour mixture into the eggs and sugar. Do not overmix once the flour is added. Fold in the melted butter with a spatula.

Scrape the batter over the apples and bake until a toothpick inserted in the center of the cake comes out clean, about 40 minutes. Cool the cake on a rack for 20 minutes. Loosen the edges of the cake with a knife and invert onto a serving plate.

COUNTRY TIPS AND TALES

Adam's Apple

History has said it was Adam's hex—
A lush red apple, the symbol of sex.
Eve was lured to taste the forbidden fruit
And the snake sneered as her spouse followed suit.
Now a botanist is bold to declare
That the apple tree did not flourish there.
The sun-laden fruit that made Adam wince
Really must have been apricot or quince!
—Roberta Butterfield Goldstein, "Fling Jeweled Pebbles"

Cinnamon Apple Coffeecake

This tender cake made with yogurt has a layer of apples nestled inside. Easily doubled, it will feed a crowd.

1¼ cups sugar

1½ teaspoons ground cinnamon

2 large apples, such as Cortland or Northern Spy, cored, peeled, and thinly sliced

½ cup (1 stick) unsalted butter, at room temperature

2 large eggs

1½ cups all-purpose flour

1½ teaspoons baking powder

½ teaspoon baking soda

¼ teaspoon salt

1 cup plain yogurt

1 teaspoon pure vanilla extract

⅔ cup finely chopped walnuts

Preheat the oven to 350°F. Grease a 9 × 13-inch baking pan. Stir together the sugar and cinnamon in a small bowl. Place the apples in another small bowl and sprinkle them with 2 tablespoons of the sugar mixture.

In a medium-size bowl, cream together the butter and the remaining sugar mixture with an electric mixer on high speed until light and fluffy. Beat in the eggs, one at a time, scraping down the sides of the bowl after each addition.

In a small bowl, stir together the flour, baking powder and soda, and salt. On low speed, add to the butter mixture alternately with the yogurt just until the flour is moistened. Stir in the vanilla and walnuts.

Spread half of the batter evenly in the pan and place the apples over it in three rows. Spoon on the remaining batter and gently spread to cover the apple slices. Bake until a toothpick inserted in the center of the cake comes out clean, about 30 minutes. Cool the cake on a rack for 20 minutes. Loosen the edge of the cake with a knife and invert onto a rack to finish cooling. Reinvert onto a serving plate.

Apple and Cheddar Pie

MAKES ONE 9-INCH PIE

New Englanders like to combine a slice of their sharp Cheddar with sweet apple pie. I decided to try baking the cheese in with the crust and the results were delicious. Everyone has their favorite type of apple for pies and I like to mix tart and sweet varieties for an interesting flavor. Some favorites are Cortland, Northern Spy, McIntosh, Lodi, greening, Macoun, Jonathan, and Granny Smith.

FOR THE PASTRY

2 cups all-purpose flour

1 tablespoon sugar

½ teaspoon salt

¼ cup (½ stick) cold unsalted butter, cut into pieces

¼ cup cold vegetable shortening

1 cup grated extra-sharp Cheddar cheese

⅓ cup cold water

FOR THE FILLING

2½ pounds mixed tart and sweet apples, cored, peeled, and cut into chunks

2 tablespoons all-purpose flour

½ cup sugar

½ teaspoon ground cinnamon

To make the crust, stir together the flour, sugar, and salt in a medium-size bowl. Cut in the butter and shortening with a pastry blender or rub it in with your fingers until the mixture resemble oatmeal. Toss in the cheese. Stir in the water with a fork until the dough gathers into a ball, adding more water if needed. Flatten into a disk, dust with flour, and cover with plastic wrap or waxed paper. Chill for 1 hour.

To make the filling, place the apples in a large bowl. Mix the flour, sugar, and cinnamon together and toss with the apples until evenly coated.

Preheat the oven to 450°F. To assemble, divide the dough in half, lightly flour a worktable, and roll out the dough with a floured rolling pin into an 11-inch circle. Drape it over the rolling pin, fit the dough into a 9-inch pie plate, and spoon in the filling. Lightly flour the table and roll out the remaining dough into an 11-inch circle.

Moisten the rim of the bottom crust with a little water and drape the pastry over the filling. Trim the pastry to a 1-inch overhang and crimp the edges with a fork. Trim off excess dough. Cut several steam vents in the top crust. Bake for 15 minutes, reduce the oven temperature to 350°F, and bake until the crust is browned and the apples are tender when pierced with a fork through a vent, 30 to 40 minutes. Cool completely on a rack before serving.

COUNTRY TIPS AND TALES

The best advice I can share about pastry dough is this: Keep it cold and keep it moving! The dough will relax and roll more easily if well chilled, and if you move the dough each time you roll it and turn it over from time to time, it will roll evenly and won't stick to the table. Use enough flour when rolling the dough to keep it from sticking and brush off any excess before you put the dough in the pie plate.

Caramel Apple Pie

MAKES ONE 9-INCH PIE

I have always loved those caramel-coated apples sold at fairs, but the fillings in my teeth don't. By combining the flavors of caramel and apples in this pie, I can have my pie and eat it!

FOR THE PASTRY

1 cup all-purpose flour

2 teaspoons sugar

½ teaspoon salt

2 tablespoons cold unsalted butter, cut into pieces

2 tablespoons cold vegetable shortening

¼ cup cold water

2 pounds tart apples, such as greening or Granny Smith, cored, peeled,
 and coarsely grated

3 large eggs, beaten

1 cup sugar

6 tablespoons (¾ stick) unsalted butter, melted

1 tablespoon dark rum

To make the dough, stir together the flour, sugar, and salt in a small bowl. Cut in the butter and shortening with a pastry blender or rub it in with your fingers until the mixture resembles oatmeal. Stir in the water with a fork until the dough gathers into a ball, adding more water if needed. Flatten into a disk, dust with flour, and cover with plastic wrap or waxed paper. Chill for 1 hour.

To make the filling, place the grated apples in a large bowl and stir in the eggs. To make the caramel, cook the sugar in a nonstick skillet over medium heat, stirring constantly, until it becomes a deep amber liquid. It will get lumpy but it gradually smooths out. Avoid touching the hot sugar syrup because it can burn. Remove from the heat, add the melted butter and rum, and beat the caramel very gradually into the apple-egg mixture with a whisk. The syrup may harden in the apple mixture. Keep stirring and it will dissolve.

Preheat the oven to 425°F. To assemble, roll out the dough on a lightly floured worktable with a floured rolling pin into an 11-inch circle. Drape it over the rolling pin and fit the dough into a 9-inch pie plate. Fold over the edges and decoratively crimp with a fork. Spoon in the filling. Bake for 15 minutes, reduce the oven temperature to 350°F, and bake until the crust is golden brown and the filling set, about 30 minutes. Cool completely on a rack before serving.

COUNTRY TIPS AND TALES

Grating apples or using applesauce for pies was common practice in New England and the Lattice-Topped Squash and Apple Pie on page 219 is another example.

Boiled Cider Tartlets

J am tarts were a part of early English cooking and the intense, winey apple flavor of boiled cider, a concentrated syrup made from apple cider, really makes these rich mouthfuls a treat. Sour cream gives a mellow taste to the flaky pastry.

The technique of folding and rolling pastry dough is called "turning" and gives the pastry extra layers of flakiness. Use mini-muffin tins or old tartlet pans like those found in New England flea markets.

FOR THE PASTRY

¾ cup all-purpose flour

½ teaspoon salt

Pinch of sugar

3 tablespoons cold unsalted butter, cut into pieces

2 tablespoons cold vegetable shortening

1 tablespoon sour cream

1 tablespoon water

FOR THE FILLING

½ cup boiled cider (see Mail-Order Sources, page 255)

2 tablespoons sugar

2 tablespoons heavy cream

2 teaspoons brandy or applejack

1 large egg

To make the dough, stir together the flour, salt, and sugar in a small bowl. Cut in the butter and shortening with a pastry blender or rub it in with your fingers until the mixture resembles oatmeal. Small lumps of butter may remain. Stir in the sour cream and water with a fork until the dough gathers into a ball. Add more water if needed. Place the dough on a lightly floured worktable and roll out the dough with a floured rolling pin into a rectangle about 5 × 8 inches. Fold into thirds like a letter and roll out again to a rectangle. Repeat this procedure once more, then cover the dough with plastic wrap or waxed paper and chill at least 1 hour.

To make the filling, in a medium-size bowl, whisk together the cider, sugar, cream, and brandy until the sugar dissolves. Beat in the egg until the mixture is well blended.

Preheat the oven to 425°F. To assemble, roll out the dough on a lightly floured worktable with a floured rolling pin until very thin. Using a 3-inch cutter, cut out circles from the dough and press them into the tartlet pans. Gather together the dough scraps, roll the dough out again, and cut out the remaining circles. Spoon some of the filling into each tartlet and bake for 10 minutes. Reduce the heat to 350°F and bake until the filling is set, another 5 minutes. Cool completely on a rack before removing from the pans.

COUNTRY TIPS AND TALES

Pie-crust making is held in high esteem by my neighbors, and the old saying "It's a poor crust that will not grease its own plate" tells how they judge each other's efforts.

Ginger-Stewed Pears

MAKES 4 SERVINGS

This is a simple and satisfying dessert to end a supper at home. Any fruit or combination of fruits can be stewed in this manner.

One 2-inch piece fresh ginger, peeled and smashed
¾ cup sugar
1 cup water
2 strips lemon rind
Juice of 1 lemon
4 firm medium-size Anjou or Bosc pears

Place the ginger, sugar, water, lemon rind and juice in a large nonreactive saucepan and bring to a boil, stirring occasionally. Cook over medium heat until slightly syrupy, about 20 minutes. Meanwhile, peel the pears, then slice them in half lengthwise and remove the cores. Place the pears in the syrup and simmer gently, turning them until they are tender when pierced with the point of a knife, about 15 minutes. Remove from the heat and let cool, occasionally spooning the syrup over the pears. Chill for several hours before serving.

COUNTRY TIPS AND TALES

I had a little nut tree, nothing it would bear
But a silver nutmeg and a golden pear;
The King of Spain's daughter came to visit me,
And all for the sake of my little nut tree.
—Nursery Rhyme

Chewy Dried-Pear Drops

MAKES 2 DOZEN COOKIES

Hazel Wetherby, a long-time family friend from Richford, remembered her Aunt Vidie Ladd's kitchen and especially her cookies. "Caraway cookies, sugar-coated sour cream cookies, a quarter-of-an-inch-thick molasses cookies, thin and crisp as a wafer, smooth and glossy as varnish, and crisscrossed with the marks of a knife, came out of the oven just perfect, with no burnt edges."

For this recipe, I use oiled kitchen shears to cut up the pears.

¼ cup whole-wheat flour

½ cup all-purpose flour

1 cup sugar

1 teaspoon baking powder

½ teaspoon ground ginger

½ teaspoon ground cinnamon

¼ teaspoon salt

1 cup diced dried pears

1 cup coarsely chopped hazelnuts or walnuts

2 large eggs

½ teaspoon pure vanilla extract

Preheat the oven to 350°F. Grease well a cookie sheet. Mix the flours, sugar, baking powder, ginger, cinnamon, and salt together in a large bowl. Toss the pears and nuts with the flour mixture. In a small bowl, whisk the eggs and the vanilla together until foamy, then fold into the flour mixture. Drop the dough by the tablespoon onto the cookie sheet. Bake, rotating the sheet halfway through the baking, until the cookies are dry to the touch and lightly browned, 8 to 9 minutes. Let cool on the cookie sheet for 2 minutes, then remove to a rack to fully cool. Store in a tightly covered container.

Stirred Pear and Rice Pudding

MAKES 6 TO 8 SERVINGS

Nothing seems homier than rice pudding, even though it has been raised to regal heights in French cuisine. *Riz a l'impératrice* is shown in *Larousse Gastronomique* surrounded by pears poached in a vanilla-scented syrup.

Simplify things by stirring dried pears and vanilla extract into the pudding. You can use leftover rice—but do not use an instant-cook rice—and skip the first part of the recipe, adding the cinnamon and lemon peel to the milk instead. You can easily snip the pears with oiled kitchen shears. Although you can serve the pudding chilled, it is at its loveliest barely warm.

2 cups water
Pinch of salt
1 cinnamon stick
One 2-inch strip lemon rind
1 cup uncooked long-grain rice
1 quart milk
½ cup sugar
1 cup diced dried pears
1 teaspoon pure vanilla extract
2 tablespoons toasted pine nuts or chopped almonds

Place the water, salt, cinnamon stick, and lemon rind in a medium-size nonreactive saucepan and bring to a boil over medium heat. Stir in the rice, return to a boil, stir, cover, and reduce the heat to very low. Cook until all the water is absorbed, about 15 minutes.

Meanwhile, heat the milk and sugar together in a large nonreactive saucepan over medium heat to simmering. Add the rice and cook slowly over low heat until most of the milk is absorbed, about 20 minutes. Remove the cinnamon stick and rind, stir in the pears and vanilla, and cook for 5 minutes. Pour into a shallow nonreactive dish and sprinkle with the nuts. Cool to barely warm before serving or, if chilling, cool, cover with plastic wrap, and refrigerate.

Pear Johnnycake

Johnnycake, or cornmeal pancake, baked in a cast-iron spider, has Native American origins. A spider is a black cast-iron pan on legs used in open-hearth baking. Nowadays, the legs are gone, but cast-iron skillets remain popular cooking pans, known for their even heat distribution and their versatility, both in and on top of the stove. Any type of pear will do for this hot corn cake, which goes so well with Town Meeting Beans and Bacon (page 40).

¼ cup (½ stick) unsalted butter

2 firm, ripe pears, peeled, cored, and sliced

⅛ teaspoon freshly grated nutmeg

1 cup all-purpose flour

¾ cup stone-ground white cornmeal

2 teaspoons baking powder

1 teaspoon baking soda

½ teaspoon salt

¾ cup milk

¼ cup pure dark amber or grade B maple syrup or honey

2 large eggs

Sour cream or crème fraîche (page 3) and maple syrup

Preheat the oven to 400°F. Heat 1 tablespoon of the butter in a 10-inch ovenproof skillet over medium heat and cook the pears, sprinkling them with the nutmeg, until barely tender, 4 to 5 minutes. Remove from the heat. Melt the remaining butter in a small saucepan and set aside to cool.

Stir together the flour, cornmeal, baking powder and soda, and salt in a medium-size bowl. Make a well in the center of the mixture and add the milk, maple syrup, eggs, and melted butter. With a fork break up the eggs and mix the liquid into the flour mixture just until moistened. Spread the batter on top of the pears and bake until golden brown and a toothpick inserted in the center of the cake comes out clean, 25 to 30 minutes. Cut into wedges and serve with sour cream and more maple syrup.

Raisin-Pear Crumb Cake

MAKES ONE 9-INCH SQUARE CAKE

Coffee breaks are better with a delicious cake like this one to bite
into. Tender and simple to make, it can enhance your baking reputa-
tion at the next bake sale.

2 cups all-purpose flour

¾ cup sugar

1½ teaspoons baking powder

½ teaspoon baking soda

1 teaspoon ground cinnamon

½ teaspoon salt

½ cup (1 stick) unsalted butter, at room temperature

½ cup coarsely chopped walnuts

1 large egg

½ cup plain yogurt

1 teaspoon pure vanilla extract

2 firm, ripe pears, peeled, cored, and diced

½ cup golden raisins

Preheat the oven to 375°F. Grease a 9-inch-square baking pan. Stir together the
flour, sugar, baking powder and soda, cinnamon, and salt in a large bowl. Rub in the
butter with your fingers until it is thoroughly blended with the flour mixture. To make

the topping, remove 1 cup of the mixture and stir in the walnuts. Set the topping aside.

Stir the egg, yogurt, and vanilla into the remaining flour mixture just until the flour is moistened. Stir in the pears and raisins. Spread the batter evenly into the pan and sprinkle the reserved topping over it, pressing it gently into the batter.

Bake until a toothpick inserted in the center of the cake comes out clean, 40 to 50 minutes. Cool completely on a rack and serve from the pan.

COUNTRY TIPS AND TALES

For streaks of red were mingled there,
Such as are a Catherine pear,
(The side that's next to the sun).
—Geoffrey Anketell Studdert-Kennedy (1883—1929), *The Goblins*

Pear Pie with Cream

MAKES ONE 9-INCH PIE

My mother-in-law, Mary, tells of her youth when men moved from farm to farm at threshing time. The women fed twenty-four men three meals a day for a week. She remembers making pie after pie, all of them baked in a wood stove, because the men ate pie with every meal, including breakfast.

FOR THE PASTRY

2 cups all-purpose flour

1 tablespoon sugar

1 teaspoon salt

¼ cup (½ stick) cold unsalted butter, cut into pieces

¼ cup cold vegetable shortening

⅓ cup cold water

2½ pounds firm, ripe pears, peeled, cored, and cut into chunks

2 tablespoons cornstarch

½ cup plus 1 tablespoon sugar

½ teaspoon ground cinnamon

¼ teaspoon freshly grated nutmeg

½ cup heavy cream

1 tablespoon milk

To make the dough, stir together the flour, sugar, and salt in a medium-size bowl. Cut in the butter and shortening with a pastry blender or rub it in with your fingers until the mixture resembles oatmeal. Stir in the water with a fork until the dough gathers into a ball. Add more water if needed. Flatten into a disk, dust with flour, and cover with plastic wrap or waxed paper. Chill for 1 hour.

To make the filling, place the pears in a large bowl. Mix the cornstarch, ½ cup of the sugar, the cinnamon, and nutmeg together and toss with the pears. Stir in the cream.

Preheat the oven to 450°F. To assemble, divide the dough in half, and roll out on a lightly floured worktable with a floured rolling pin into an 11-inch circle. Drape over the rolling pin, fit the dough into a 9-inch pie plate, and spoon in the filling. Lightly flour the surface, roll out the remaining dough, and cut into ten ½-inch-wide strips. Arrange the strips over the filling, weaving them in and out for a lattice pattern. Trim the pastry to a 1-inch overhang and decoratively crimp the edges with a fork. Brush the lattice with the milk and sprinkle with the remaining tablespoon of sugar.

Bake the pie for 15 minutes, reduce the oven temperature to 350°F, and bake until the crust is browned and the pears are tender when pierced with a fork, about 30 minutes. Cool completely on a rack before serving.

COUNTRY TIPS AND TALES

For pies, cakes, and white bread the heat of the [wood] oven should be such that you can hold your hand and arm while you count to 40; for brown bread, meats, beans, Indian puddings and pumpkin pies, it should be hotter, so that you can only hold it in while you count to 20.

—From an 1845 cookbook, in Molly Harrison, *The Kitchen in History*

Pear-Mincemeat Pie

MAKES 3 QUARTS OR ENOUGH FILLING FOR FOUR 9-INCH PIES

A delicious mincemeat can be made from pears and no meat, according to Jane Quigley, my baking cohort at Spring Lake Ranch. She proved how right she was by making this pie for our Christmas meal when everyone contributed desserts.

You will find it lighter and more intriguing in flavor than anything available commercially. Make the filling weeks ahead and this pie is a snap. Actually, the mincemeat improves with the wait. If you would like to add brandy or rum, do it after cooking the mincemeat, though the flavor is fine without it.

You will need 4 cups of mincemeat for a 9-inch deep-dish pie. The remaining mincemeat will keep for several months in the refrigerator or freeze it in 4-cup portions.

FOR THE MINCEMEAT

5 pounds firm, ripe pears, peeled, cored, and diced

3 pounds seedless green grapes, stems removed

1 pound golden raisins

6 cups sugar

1 cup cider vinegar

2 lemons, halved, seeded, and finely chopped, rinds and all

2 teaspoons ground cinnamon

2 teaspoons ground cloves

1 teaspoon freshly grated nutmeg

1 teaspoon ground ginger

½ cup (1 stick) unsalted butter

FOR THE PASTRY

2 cups all-purpose flour

1 tablespoon sugar

1 teaspoon salt

¼ cup (½ stick) cold unsalted butter, cut into pieces

¼ cup cold vegetable shortening

⅓ cup cold water

Combine all the mincemeat ingredients in a large nonreactive saucepan and stir well. Bring to a boil over medium heat. Reduce the heat to medium-low and cook, stirring occasionally, until thickened, about 3 hours. Cool and store in a covered container in the refrigerator for at least 2 weeks before using.

To make the dough, stir together the flour, sugar, and salt in a medium-size bowl. Cut in the butter and shortening with a pastry blender or rub it in with your fingers until the mixture resembles oatmeal. Stir in the water with a fork until the dough gathers into a ball. Flatten into a disk, dust with flour, cover with plastic wrap or waxed paper, and chill for 1 hour.

Preheat the oven to 425°F. To assemble, divide the dough in half. Roll out on a lightly floured worktable with a floured rolling pin into an 11-inch circle. Drape it over the rolling pin, fit the dough into a 9½-inch deep-dish pie plate, and spoon in the mincemeat. Roll out the remaining dough into an 11-inch circle. Drape it over the filling. Trim off the excess dough and crimp the edges with a fork. Cut several steam vents in the top crust.

Bake for 15 minutes, reduce the oven temperature to 375°F, and bake until the pastry is golden, about 30 minutes more. Cool completely on a rack before serving.

COUNTRY TIPS AND TALES

. . . when summer company was expected or when
extra haymakers or threshers were working on the farm,
pie-making went into mass production. Rows and rows
of pies with several sorts of fillings would stand
in the cool "screen cupboard" in the summer kitchen,
or in the hottest weather, on the shelves of the
airy milkroom on the north end of the deep, cool cellar.

—Dorothy Walter, *Green Mountain Whittlin's*

Pear Galette

MAKES ONE 10-INCH TART

Originally hearth-baked in a flat girdle (griddle) suspended from a hook over the fire, this rustic, free-form tart with a flaky crust is now made on a baking sheet or a pizza pan. Like most pastries, a galette is best eaten when freshly made. This calls for semolina, a granular wheat flour available in health food stores.

FOR THE DOUGH

¾ cup all-purpose flour

½ teaspoon salt

Pinch of sugar

3 tablespoons cold unsalted butter, cut into pieces

2 tablespoons cold vegetable shortening

1 tablespoon sour cream

1 tablespoon cold water

FOR THE FILLING

1 tablespoon semolina

2 tablespoons finely ground unblanched almonds

6 firm, ripe Anjou pears, peeled, cored, and cut into thin slices

3 tablespoons sugar

To make the dough, stir the flour, salt, and sugar together in a small bowl. Cut in the butter and shortening with a pastry blender or two knives or rub it in with your fingers until the mixture resembles oatmeal. Small lumps of butter may remain. Stir in the sour cream and water with a fork until the dough gathers into a ball. Place the dough on a lightly floured worktable and with a floured rolling pin, roll out the dough into a rectangle about 4 × 6 inches. Fold it into thirds like a letter, then roll into another 4 × 6-inch rectangle. Repeat this procedure once more, then cover the dough with plastic wrap or waxed paper and chill at least 1 hour.

Preheat the oven to 375°F. To assemble, roll out the dough on a lightly floured worktable with a floured rolling pin into a 12-inch circle. Drape it over the rolling pin and lift onto a large baking sheet. Mix the semolina with the almonds and sprinkle over the dough, leaving a 2-inch border. Lay the pears in slightly overlapping circles on the semolina mixture. Sprinkle the pears with the sugar, fold the 2-inch border, pleating the dough to fit snugly over the pears. Bake until the pastry is golden brown and the pears are tender when pierced with a fork, about 30 minutes.

Cool completely on the baking sheet. Then slide the galette onto a serving plate.

COUNTRY TIPS AND TALES

One of the best baking secrets is to use a
spoonful of semolina under juicy fruits. It absorbs
any moisture without interfering with texture or flavor.
Once when I ran out of semolina, I used Cream of Wheat
cereal and while it absorbed the moisture from the fruit,
it remained a bit gritty.

Poutine aux Fraises et Bluets

MAKES 6 TO 8 SERVINGS

A warm fruit pudding made with strawberries and blueberries from Quebec, noted in *Goûter à l'histoire* by Lafrance and Desloges, it is reminiscent of clafoutis from the Limousin region in France. A similar pudding is still served in some French-Canadian homes two hundred years later.

2 cups thickly sliced hulled fresh strawberries
2 cups fresh blueberries, washed, patted dry, and stemmed
½ cup plus 2 tablespoons sugar
2 tablespoons unsalted butter, melted and cooled
1 large egg
½ teaspoon pure vanilla extract
Pinch of salt
1 cup all-purpose flour
1 teaspoon baking powder
⅔ cup milk
Heavy cream

Preheat the oven to 350°F. Place the berries in a deep, nonreactive 9-inch pie plate and sprinkle with 2 tablespoons of the sugar. Place the remaining ½ cup sugar in a medium-size bowl and whisk in the butter, egg, vanilla, and salt until the mixture is smooth and creamy. Stir the flour and baking powder together, then add to the egg mixture, alternating with the milk.

Spoon the batter over the berries and bake until the topping is golden brown, about 40 minutes. Serve hot, warm, or cold with cream.

Strawberry and Currant Spoon Pudding

MAKES 4 SERVINGS

In the *Pioneer Cook Book*, a lovely volume from Decorah, Iowa's Norwegian-American community, you will find many soft fruit puddings. They make refreshing desserts, which can be successfully made with frozen fruits. Inspired, I went currant picking and combined these glistening little berries with the last of the local strawberries. Currants are tart, reminiscent of pomegranate seeds. Substitute fresh raspberries if currants are unavailable.

4 cups fresh red currants, washed, patted dry, and stemmed

2 cups thickly sliced hulled fresh strawberries

1 cup sugar

3 tablespoons arrowroot or cornstarch

1 cup water

Plain yogurt, sour cream, or crème fraîche (page 3)

Toss the berries with the sugar and arrowroot in a medium-size nonreactive saucepan and let sit at room temperature for 2 hours, until the fruits release juices. Add the water and cook, stirring often, over medium heat until boiling. Boil for 1 minute, then pour into a serving bowl, covering the top with plastic wrap to prevent a skin from forming. Chill for several hours before serving. Serve with yogurt, sour cream, or crème fraîche.

COUNTRY TIPS AND TALES

Always wash strawberries before hulling.
This prevents the berries from becoming waterlogged.

Strawberry-Rhubarb Crisp

Whoever first combined strawberries and rhubarb was an inspired cook. Rhubarb grows so well in northern gardens and many cooks' reputations rest on their rhubarb or strawberry-rhubarb pie. The sweet-tart flavors come through in this dessert, coated with an almond-studded sugar topping. This can be made with any fruit or combination of fruits and any type of nut. Remember to use only the stalks of the rhubarb, as the leaf is poisonous!

FOR THE FRUIT

2 cups thickly sliced hulled fresh strawberries

2 cups coarsely chopped rhubarb stalks

¼ cup sugar

1 tablespoon cornstarch

2 teaspoons tapioca

FOR THE TOPPING

¾ cup all-purpose flour

¾ cup sugar

½ cup coarsely chopped almonds, skins on

½ cup (1 stick) unsalted butter

Heavy cream or plain yogurt

Preheat the oven to 375°F. Place the strawberries, rhubarb, sugar, cornstarch, and tapioca in a medium-size nonreactive saucepan and cook over medium heat, stirring occasionally, until the mixture comes to a boil and is thickened, 10 to 12 minutes. Pour into a nonreactive 9½-inch deep-dish pie plate.

Place the flour, sugar, almonds, and butter in a medium-size bowl and rub together with your fingers until the butter is thoroughly blended. The mixture will be lumpy. Sprinkle evenly over the fruit mixture and bake until the topping is golden brown, about 25 minutes. Serve warm with cream or yogurt.

Baked Sour-Cherry Flan

Trish Norton of Cuttingsville cans sour cherries with maple syrup for pie making in the winter months. Neither her trees nor mine are big enough to yield enough cherries to bake even a single pie, and we go to two area orchards to pick sour cherries. This year, I made lots of my all-time favorite sour cherry preserves. The leftover cherries went into this easy, old-fashioned dessert. Lacking an official cherry pitter, you can use a paper clip to scoop out the pits. A dollop of crème fraîche or yogurt goes on top of the flan, if you like.

2 cups pitted sour cherries

½ cup granulated sugar

2 large eggs

1 cup milk

2 tablespoons kirschwasser or brandy

½ teaspoon pure vanilla extract

Pinch of salt

1 cup all-purpose flour

2 tablespoons unsalted butter, melted

Confectioners' sugar

continued

Preheat the oven to 400°F. Butter a nonreactive 9-inch pie plate and place the cherries evenly in the pan. Sprinkle with 3 tablespoons of the sugar. Place the remaining 5 tablespoons sugar in a medium-size bowl and whisk in the eggs until well combined. Whisk in the milk, kirschwasser, vanilla, and salt. Add the flour gradually and stir until smooth. Stir in the butter. Pour the batter over the cherries and bake until the edges are browned and the flan is puffed, about 30 minutes. Remove from the oven and sprinkle heavily with confectioners' sugar. Cool for 10 minutes before serving from the pan.

Strawberry Dumplings

MAKES 4 TO 6 SERVINGS

On a sunny Saturday towards the end of June, Len and I went strawberry picking at one of the local farms, because I had promised to replicate the strawberry dumplings of his childhood. He has memories of the family putting up quarts of strawberries in waxed paper containers for the freezer, and their reward was strawberry dumplings, a once-a-year treat.

4 cups thickly sliced hulled fresh strawberries
½ to ⅔ cup sugar, depending on sweetness of berries
1 cup all-purpose flour
2 teaspoons baking powder
¼ teaspoon salt
1½ tablespoons vegetable shortening
⅔ cup milk
Heavy cream or crème fraîche (page 3)

Place the berries and sugar in a medium-size nonreactive saucepan and bring to a boil over medium heat, stirring occasionally. Place the flour, baking powder, and salt in a bowl and rub in the shortening with your fingers until the mixture resembles oatmeal. Stir in the milk and scrape the mixture into the boiling berries. Stir well, cover the saucepan, reduce the heat to low, and cook the pudding until it looks dry on top, 10 to 15 minutes. Pour it into a bowl to serve with cream or crème fraîche.

COUNTRY TIPS AND TALES

The man in the wilderness asked me,
How many strawberries grow in the sea?
I answered him, as I thought good,
As many as red herrings grow in the wood.

—Nursery Rhyme

Blackberry Sugar Tart

MAKES ONE 9- OR 9½-INCH TART

The last berry to arrive on the summer scene is the blackberry. It is the hardest to pick because the thorny bushes hide away in the woods, but the berries seem more precious for the effort. Blackberry wine, or cordial, has been made since the late 1600s and is sipped by little old ladies for medicinal purposes. The pastry for this tart is a buttery cookie crust, perfect for containing the juices of the berries.

FOR THE PASTRY

1½ cups all-purpose flour

½ cup sugar

1 teaspoon baking powder

½ cup (1 stick) cold unsalted butter, cut into pieces

1 large egg

1 teaspoon pure vanilla extract

FOR THE FILLING

5 cups fresh blackberries

½ cup sugar

2 tablespoons cornstarch

1 tablespoon tapioca

To make the dough, stir together the flour, sugar, and baking powder in a medium-size bowl. Cut in the butter with a pastry blender or rub it into the flour with your fingers until the mixture resembles oatmeal. Stir in the egg and vanilla with a fork until the dough gathers into a ball, adding water, if needed. With floured fingertips, press the dough against the bottom and sides of an ungreased 9- or 9½-inch springform pan. Chill for 10 minutes.

Preheat the oven to 350°F. To prepare the filling, toss the berries in a bowl with the sugar, cornstarch, and tapioca. Place them in the pan, loosely cover the tart with a sheet of aluminum foil, and place the pan on a cookie sheet on the oven rack; the sheet will catch any drips from bubbling up berry juices. Bake until the berries are bubbling and the crust is browned, 50 to 60 minutes. Cool on a rack for 20 minutes before removing the sides of the pan.

Fresh Currant Pie

MAKES ONE 9-INCH PIE

Currants make a tangy pie and it is a shame that they are almost unused by most people. The colonists cultivated European currants for fruit and wines even though a wild variety existed and was used by the Native Americans. I have planted five currant bushes behind my house, and look forward to the day they will yield enough berries for a pie. Happily, just over the state line in New York there is a pick-your-own berry farm with loads of shiny currants waiting to be harvested. If no currants are available, substitute another berry and adjust the sugar to the sweetness of the berries.

FOR THE PASTRY
2 cups all-purpose flour

1 tablespoon sugar

1 teaspoon salt

¼ cup (½ stick) cold unsalted butter, cut into pieces

¼ cup cold vegetable shortening

⅓ cup cold water

FOR THE FILLING
6 cups fresh currants, washed, patted dry, and stemmed

1⅓ cups plus 1 tablespoon sugar

2 tablespoons cornstarch

2 tablespoons tapioca

1 tablespoon milk

To mix the dough, stir together the flour, sugar, and salt in a medium-size bowl. Cut in the butter and shortening with a pastry blender or rub it into the flour with your fingers until the mixture resembles oatmeal. Stir in the water with a fork until the dough gathers into a ball. Flatten into a disk, dust with flour, and cover the dough with plastic wrap or waxed paper. Chill for 1 hour.

To make the filling, place the currants in a large bowl. Mix together 1⅓ cups of the sugar, the cornstarch, and tapioca and toss with the currants.

continued

Preheat the oven to 450°F. To assemble, divide the dough in half and roll out on a lightly floured worktable with a floured rolling pin into an 11-inch circle. Drape it over the rolling pin, fit the dough into a 9-inch pie plate, and spoon in the filling. Lightly flour the work surface and roll out the remaining dough into an 11-inch circle. Moisten the rim of the bottom crust with a little water and place the top crust over the currants. Trim the pastry to a 1-inch overhang; fold the edges and crimp together with a fork. Cut several steam vents in the top crust. Brush the crust with the milk and sprinkle with the remaining tablespoon sugar.

Set the pan on a cookie sheet to catch spills. Bake for 15 minutes, reduce the oven temperature to 350°F, and bake until the crust is golden brown and the filling is bubbling, about 40 minutes longer. Cool completely on a rack before serving.

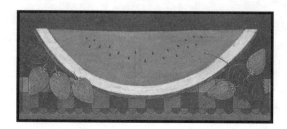

Shortcake with Vanilla Blueberry Sauce

MAKES 4 TO 6 SERVINGS

By the time July is halfway through, I am impatient for my blueberries to ripen. If you have a sunny, moist spot in your garden, plant a few bushes. They are easy to grow, to pick, and to eat. You can make individual biscuits from this shortcake recipe or serve it whole and cut into wedges. We ate a lovely blueberry crisp at the supper in Newfane. The folks at the table enjoyed going to the suppers, not only to support their community, but also because they did not have to cook that night!

FOR THE SHORTCAKE

2 cups all-purpose flour

⅓ cup plus 1 tablespoon sugar

1 tablespoon baking powder

½ teaspoon baking soda

½ teaspoon salt

7 tablespoons unsalted butter

1 large egg yolk

⅔ cup buttermilk

FOR THE VANILLA BLUEBERRY SAUCE

3 cups fresh blueberries, washed, patted dry, and stemmed

½ cup sugar

½ cup vanilla bean or 1 teaspoon pure vanilla extract

FOR THE WHIPPED CREAM

1 cup heavy cream

¼ cup sugar

½ teaspoon pure vanilla extract

Preheat the oven to 400°F. To prepare the shortcake, grease an 8-inch cake pan. Stir together the flour, ⅓ cup sugar, the baking powder and soda, and salt in a medium bowl. Cut in 6 tablespoons of the butter with a pastry blender or rub it in with your fingers until the mixture resembles oatmeal. Stir in the egg yolk and buttermilk with a fork to make a soft dough. Pat the dough flat in the pan. Melt the remaining tablespoon butter and brush on top of the shortcake. Sprinkle with the remaining tablespoon sugar and bake until golden, about 25 minutes. Cool for 15 minutes in the pan, then invert onto a rack to finish cooling. Remove the pan and reinvert the cake sugar side up.

Meanwhile, prepare the sauce by combining the berries, sugar, and vanilla bean in a small nonreactive 1-quart saucepan. If you are using the vanilla extract, stir it in after the berries cook. Cover and cook slowly over low heat until juicy, about 20 minutes. Remove from the heat, discard the vanilla bean, and cool the sauce until barely warm.

Whip the cream with the sugar and vanilla in a medium-size bowl on medium-high speed until soft peaks form. Place the shortcake on a serving platter. Assemble the cake by slicing the shortcake in half horizontally. Spoon the sauce over the bottom half of the cake and spoon the cream on the sauce. Carefully place the top half of the cake on the cream. Cut into wedges to serve.

Blueberry Coffeecake

MAKES 12 SERVINGS

Even if I did not grow blueberries, I would make this cake for its fine flavor and aroma. When this homey cake is baking, people come sniffing around and smiling. You must convince them to wait until the cake has cooled. If you want to use frozen blueberries, do not defrost them, or your cake will be soggy.

1½ cups all-purpose flour
½ cup whole-wheat flour
¾ cup sugar
1½ teaspoons baking powder
½ teaspoon baking soda
½ teaspoon salt
½ teaspoon ground cinnamon
¼ teaspoon freshly grated nutmeg
½ cup (1 stick) unsalted butter
1 large egg
½ cup plain yogurt
1 teaspoon pure vanilla extract
2 cups fresh blueberries, washed, patted dry, and stemmed

Preheat the oven to 375°F. Grease a 10-inch-square baking pan. Stir together the flours, sugar, baking powder and soda, salt, cinnamon, and nutmeg in a large bowl. Rub in the butter with your fingers until the mixture resembles oatmeal. Remove 1 cup of the mixture and set aside.

With a fork, stir in the egg, yogurt, and vanilla just until the flour is moistened. Gently stir in the blueberries. Spread the batter in the cake pan and sprinkle evenly with the reserved crumb mixture. Bake until golden brown and a toothpick inserted in the center of the cake comes out clean, 40 to 50 minutes. Cool for 20 minutes on a rack. Cut into 12 pieces and serve warm from the pan.

Raspberry Topsy-Turvy

MAKES 6 TO 8 SERVINGS

There is a sense of excitement when making an upside-down cake. Although you know what you have put into the cake, when it is inverted onto your serving plate, it seems much more than the sum of its parts. Making this upside-down cake gives you a juicy, berry-soaked cake that should and will be eaten up quickly. Serve it with ice cream or whipped cream—or plain cream, if you must.

3 cups fresh raspberries

1 cup sugar

3 large eggs

1 teaspoon pure vanilla extract

¼ teaspoon salt

⅔ cup all-purpose flour

2 tablespoons unsalted butter, melted

Preheat the oven to 350°F. Butter a nonreactive 9-inch cake pan and spread the raspberries evenly in the pan. Sprinkle with ⅓ cup of the sugar. In a large bowl, beat the remaining ⅔ cup sugar together with the eggs, vanilla, and salt with an electric mixer on high speed until the mixture is pale and very thick, about 5 minutes. With the mixer on the lowest speed, stir in the flour, then the melted butter. Do not overmix. Pour the batter over the raspberries and bake until the cake is well browned and a tester inserted into the center of the cake comes out clean, about 40 minutes. Cool for 20 minutes on a rack. Loosen the sides of the cake with a knife and invert onto a serving plate.

> ### COUNTRY TIPS AND TALES
>
> Come elf and fairy and summer sprites
> With the nectar that summer brings
> From the fairest fruits and berries ripe
> And juice of a thousand things.
>
> —Marthas Vineyard Hospital, *Island Cook Book*

Len's Blueberry Pancakes

MAKES TWELVE 3-INCH PANCAKES

Some evenings we are both too tired to be creative and want a simple, quick supper. Len makes these pancakes in no time, and they are delicious and satisfying. Of course you can make them for breakfast, too. Pure maple syrup is the only topping needed. If you have fresh buttermilk, use 1 cup instead of the dried buttermilk and water. If using frozen berries, regulate the heat of the griddle so as not to overcook the pancakes before the berries thaw.

½ cup all-purpose flour

½ cup whole-wheat flour

¼ cup buttermilk powder

1 tablespoon sugar

1 teaspoon baking powder

½ teaspoon baking soda

¼ teaspoon salt

¼ teaspoon ground cinnamon

1 large egg

2 tablespoons canola oil

1 cup water

1½ cups fresh blueberries, washed, patted dry, and stemmed, or unthawed frozen blueberries

Preheat the oven to the lowest possible setting and warm an ovenproof serving dish. Stir together the flours, buttermilk powder, sugar, baking powder and soda, salt, and cinnamon in a large bowl. Make a well in the flour mixture and put in the egg, oil, and water. Break up the egg with a fork and stir everything together until smooth.

Heat a griddle or nonstick frying pan over medium-low heat until hot. Spray with cooking spray or wipe with a greased paper towel. Pour ¼ cup batter for each pancake and cook for 2 minutes. Place about 8 berries on each pancake. Cook until bubbles appear on top and the edges are browned. Flip over to brown the other side. Place the cooked pancakes on the plate in the oven and cover loosely with a sheet of aluminum foil until all the pancakes are cooked.

Quince Preserves

MAKES 4 HALF-PINT JARS

A bowl of yellow quinces sitting on the table brings the sweetest aroma into the kitchen. That's how you tell they are ripe—they're almost perfumed. Quinces turn a beautiful golden-rosy color when cooked and are delicious used as a glaze for roast pork or spooned over fresh ricotta cheese.

My friend Ralph Stieber knows I love quinces, and one Christmas gave me a jar of these preserves. We really laughed when I pulled out a jar of the same preserves to give to him.

3 pounds ripe quinces, peeled, cored, and cut into thin slices
3 cups sugar
2 strips lemon rind (about 1 × 3 inches long)
1 cup water

Sterilize the jars and lids by placing them in a deep soup or canning kettle with a rack in the bottom. Cover with water and bring to a boil. Let sit in the water off the heat while you prepare the preserves.

Combine the quinces, sugar, lemon strips, and water in a large nonreactive saucepan and bring to a boil over medium heat. Reduce the heat to low and cook slowly, stirring occasionally, until the quinces are translucent and the liquid is syrupy, 1½ to 2 hours.

Drain the jars and lids on a clean kitchen towel. Pour the preserves into the sterilized jars, leaving ¼ inch head space. Wipe the rims clean and seal the jars. Place the jars on a rack in a large pot of boiling water. The water should come 2 inches above the jars. Run a knife around the insides of each jar to release any air bubbles. Tightly cover the pot when the water is boiling and boil for 10 minutes. Remove the jars and cool them on kitchen towels. If properly sealed, the jars will ping as they cool down and the tops become concave. Cool for 12 hours and check the seals. Store any jars in the refrigerator that did not seal properly and eat those preserves first. Store the others in a cool, dark place. Refrigerate after opening.

COUNTRY TIPS AND TALES

One of the most ancient fruits, the quince has practically slipped into oblivion in this country. Old cookbooks have recipes for quince pies and Middle Eastern and Greek cuisines still use the fruit as a spoon sweet. Marmalade is said to be originally made of quince, which the Portuguese call *marmela*. *The Housekeeper's Book* by A Lady is a funny little book written in 1837 by an anonymous woman who was very knowledgeable.
She wrote in her recipe for apple pie, "some slices of quince are a great improvement, or quince marmalade. . . ."

Blueberry Preserves

MAKES 6 OR 7 HALF-PINT JARS

Now that our children are grown, our blueberry bushes produce far more than two people can eat. So I make up preserves to give away as gifts when I am invited to someone's house for supper. Since blueberries freeze well, if I run out of preserves during the winter, it is easy to make a new batch. If you are interested in canning, the *Ball Blue Book* is a helpful guide to take you through the complete process.

5 pounds fresh blueberries, about 10 cups, washed, patted dry,
stemmed, and crushed
6 cups sugar
Juice of 4 lemons

Sterilize the jars and lids by placing them in a deep soup or canning kettle with a rack in the bottom. Cover with water and bring to a boil. Let sit in the water off the heat while you prepare the preserves.

Combine the berries, sugar, and lemon juice in a large nonreactive saucepan and bring to a boil over medium heat. Cook, stirring occasionally, until the temperature reaches 224°F on a candy thermometer.

Drain the jars and lids on a clean kitchen towel. Pour the preserves into the sterilized jars, leaving ¼ inch of head space. Wipe the rims clean and seal the jars. Place the jars on a rack in a large pot of boiling water. The water should come 2 inches above the jars. Run a knife around the insides of each jar to release any air bubbles. Tightly cover the pot when the water is boiling and boil for 10 minutes. Remove the jars and cool them on kitchen towels. If properly sealed, the jars will ping as they cool down and the tops become concave. Cool for 12 hours and check the seals. Store any jars in the refrigerator that did not seal properly and eat those preserves first. Store the others in a cool, dark place. Refrigerate after opening.

COUNTRY TIPS AND TALES

To make sure all the bacteria on the lids are killed, turn the jars over for a few minutes when you remove them from the canner after processing.

Strawberry-Rhubarb Preserves

MAKES 5 HALF-PINT JARS

We transplanted a huge clump of rhubarb from the lower garden at Spring Lake Ranch and it immediately took to our soil. I love having the rhubarb to make many dishes, including this spread of sweet berries and tart rhubarb. It is perfect for toast or waffles and delicious spooned over a scoop of vanilla ice cream for a midwinter treat.

2 pounds fresh strawberries, hulled
1½ pounds rhubarb stalks, cut into 1-inch chunks
2 cups sugar

Sterilize the jars and lids by placing them in a deep soup or canning kettle with a rack in the bottom. Cover with water and bring to a boil. Let sit in the water off the heat while you prepare the preserves.

Combine the berries, rhubarb, and sugar in a large nonreactive saucepan and bring to a boil over medium heat. Reduce the heat to low and cook, stirring often, until thickened, about 1 hour.

Drain the jars and lids on a clean kitchen towel. Pour the preserves into the sterilized jars, leaving ¼ inch of head space. Wipe the rims clean and seal the jars. Place the jars on a rack in a large pot of boiling water. The water should come 2 inches above the jars. Run a knife around the insides of each jar to release any air bubbles. Tightly cover the pot when the water is boiling and boil for 10 minutes. Remove the jars and cool them on kitchen towels. If properly sealed, the jars will ping as they cool down and the tops become concave. Cool for 12 hours and check the seals. Refrigerate those jars that don't seal properly and eat the contents right away. Store the others in a cool, dark place. Refrigerate after opening.

COUNTRY TIPS AND TALES

Frozen rhubarb and strawberries need to be thawed before making preserves. Make it simple by freezing the fruit in the amounts you will need to make your favorite recipes.

Mary's Brown-Sugar Seckels

MAKES 4 PINTS

My mother-in-law, Mary Cousineau, is a wonderful gardener, and she taught me how to can fruits and vegetables. She had a Seckel pear tree in her yard and made these dark, sweet pear preserves, delicious served with heavy or sour cream. Seckel pears appear in the supermarkets briefly in the fall. I find the firm Bosc pears make good substitutes.

3 cups firmly packed dark brown sugar
5½ cups water
5 pounds Seckel pears, peeled, halved, and cored

Sterilize the jars and lids by placing them in a deep soup or canning kettle with a rack in the bottom. Cover with water and bring to a boil. Let sit in the water off the heat.

In a large nonreactive saucepan, cook the sugar and water together over medium heat, stirring, until the sugar is dissolved. Do not boil. Stir in the pears and cook for 5 minutes.

Drain the jars and lids on a clean kitchen towel. Remove the pears from the saucepan with a slotted spoon and put them in the sterilized jars. Bring the syrup to a boil and pour over the pears, leaving ¼ inch of head space. Wipe the rims clean and seal the jars. Place the jars on a rack in a large pot of boiling water. The water should come 2 inches above the jars. Tightly cover the pot when the water is boiling and boil for 20 minutes. Remove the jars and cool them on kitchen towels. If properly sealed, the jars will ping as they cool down and the tops become concave. Refrigerate those jars that don't seal properly and eat the contents right away. Store the others in a cool, dark place. Refrigerate after opening. Serve with a pitcher of heavy or sour cream.

Spiced Apple Butter

MAKES ABOUT 8½ PINTS

Besides drying apples, pressing cider, and storing fresh apples in the cold cellar, making fragrant apple butter was another way to preserve the abundant apple crop. Try spreading this butter on Rob's Raisin Whole-Wheat Bread (page 111) for as satisfying a snack as can be. Remember to stir frequently while cooking the apple butter to prevent scorching. Invite some friends over to share the stirring and the apple butter.

> 6 pounds tart, flavorful apples, such as McIntosh or Cortland,
>   quartered
> 2 quarts sweet apple cider
> 3 cups firmly packed light brown sugar
> 2 cinnamon sticks

Sterilize the jars and lids by placing them in a deep soup or canning kettle with a rack in the bottom. Cover with water and bring to a boil. Let sit in the water off the heat.

Place the apples and cider in a large, heavy-bottomed nonreactive saucepan, cover, and cook over medium heat until the apples are tender, 35 to 40 minutes. Press the mixture through a sieve or a food mill and return to the cleaned saucepan. Cook over medium heat until thick enough to mound in a spoon, stirring frequently. Add the sugar and cinnamon sticks and cook over low heat, stirring often, for about 3 hours. Remove the cinnamon sticks.

Drain the jars and lids on a clean kitchen towel. Pour the butter into the sterilized jars, leaving ¼ inch of head space. Wipe the rims clean and seal the jars. Place them on a rack in a large pot of boiling water. The water should come 2 inches above the jars. Tightly cover the pot when the water is boiling and boil for 10 minutes. Remove the jars and cool them on kitchen towels. If properly sealed, the jars will ping as they cool down and the tops become concave. Refrigerate those jars that don't seal properly and eat the contents right away. Store the others in a cool, dark place. Refrigerate after opening.

COUNTRY TIPS AND TALES

To preserve the flavor of the fruit when making fruit butters, it is important not to use too much spice during the cooking.

Pumpkin, Squash, and Maple Desserts

IN MID-SEPTEMBER WHEN THE farmers begin to cut their corn for silage, the pumpkins appear. I know then that summer is ending and it is time to clean up the garden. Pumpkins only stay in the markets for about eight weeks.

Nearby Rutland is a city that takes Halloween seriously, with a famous parade with many costumed participants. Of course, one must have scads and scads of pumpkins to light the way. And for your information, this year's Biggest Pumpkin at the State Fair only weighed a measly 290 pounds. Last year's weighed 450.

Pumpkins really don't keep as well as other winter squashes and those may be used interchangeably with them in cooking. While most people only think of using pumpkin for pumpkin pie, it can be cooked in many savory ways, from ravioli stuffing to velvety soups. The golden flesh combines well with fresh chiles and Parmesan cheese. I actually prefer butternut and Hubbard squashes for baking, because they have a lower water content than pumpkin.

The Abenaki Indians taught the early Vermonters to boil down the maple sap to make maple syrup, which they used to sweeten pumpkins and squash. Pure Vermont maple syrup became an important source of revenue, as it remains today.

Making syrup, or sugaring, begins at the end of winter when it's still too early for the farmer to work in the fields. It takes long hours and hard work to produce maple syrup, requiring forty gallons of sap to make a gallon of syrup, so you can see why it is so expensive. Every year the sap is different and the sugarmaker never knows what the yield of each grade will be until the boiling is finished. The grading of syrup is now state controlled and there are strict standards to meet before selling the syrup. The different grades are a reflection of the sugar content in the sap.

The housewife of the past used maple sugar, which she grated from a block for baking, or melted in water if she needed syrup. (Maple sugar is syrup cooked until crystallization occurs.) Often supper consisted of cornmeal mush with milk and maple sugar. We still celebrate the first finished syrup by drizzling some on a patch of clean snow and eating this with pickles and doughnuts. When sugaring is over, mud season starts, which is Vermont's answer to spring.

Nutmeg-Squash Cookies

MAKES 2 DOZEN 3-INCH COOKIES

Tender and flavorful, these moist cookies are one of those sneaky ways mothers get their kids to eat squash. We call them "squashed cookies" because they start off high and end up flat.

1½ cups all-purpose flour
1 teaspoon baking powder
½ teaspoon baking soda
¼ teaspoon freshly grated nutmeg
¼ teaspoon salt
½ cup (1 stick) unsalted butter, at room temperature

1 cup firmly packed light brown sugar

½ teaspoon pure vanilla extract

2 large eggs

2 cups peeled and grated squash

½ cup raisins or dried cranberries (or ¼ cup each)

½ cup coarsely chopped walnuts

Preheat the oven to 350°F. Grease two cookie sheets or use parchment paper to line a baking sheet. Stir together the flour, baking powder and soda, nutmeg, and salt in a small bowl. In a large bowl, cream the butter, sugar, and vanilla together with an electric mixer on high speed until light and fluffy. Add the eggs, one at a time, scraping down the sides of the bowl after each addition. On low speed, mix in the flour mixture, the squash, raisins, and nuts just until combined. Do not overmix.

Using 2 tablespoons of the dough for each cookie, drop onto the baking sheet, spacing the cookies 2 inches apart; they will spread. Bake until the cookies are browned around the edges and feel spongy to the touch, about 17 minutes. Cool for 10 minutes before removing from the sheet.

The cookies get soggy if tightly covered, so store them on a rack loosely covered with aluminum foil.

COUNTRY TIPS AND TALES

If you do a great deal of cookie baking, it is worthwhile investing in several heavy-duty baking sheets—but make sure they will fit in your oven. Some pans are 17 inches long and too long for some ovens.

Pumpkin Date Loaf

MAKES 2 LOAVES

This tea bread is delicious with any bean supper. Wrapped well, it freezes beautifully.

⅔ cup all-purpose flour

⅓ cup whole-wheat flour

⅓ cup cornmeal

1½ teaspoons baking powder

½ teaspoon baking soda

½ teaspoon ground cinnamon

¼ teaspoon ground allspice

¼ teaspoon salt

6 tablespoons (¾ stick) unsalted butter, at room temperature

⅔ cup firmly packed dark brown sugar

2 large eggs

¾ cup fresh or canned pumpkin puree

⅓ cup buttermilk

½ cup chopped fresh or dried dates

Preheat the oven to 350°F. Grease two 7 × 4 × 2-inch loaf pans. Stir together the flours, cornmeal, baking powder and soda, spices, and salt in a small bowl. In a large bowl, cream the butter and sugar together with an electric mixer on high speed until light and fluffy. Beat in the eggs, one at a time, scraping down the sides of the bowl after each addition. On low speed, mix in the pumpkin. Stir in the flour mixture alternately with the buttermilk. Stir in the dates and scrape the batter into the loaf pans. Bake until a toothpick inserted in the center of the loaves comes out clean, about 1¼ hours.

Cool for 30 minutes in the pan. Loosen the edges of the loaves with a knife and invert on a rack. Remove the pans and carefully reinvert the loaves to finish cooling.

COUNTRY TIPS AND TALES

To make pumpkin or squash puree, cut the vegetable in half or quarters if large. Then scoop out the seeds, place cut side down in a roasting pan with ½ inch water, cover with aluminum foil, and bake in a preheated 400°F oven until the flesh is tender, about 1 hour. Cool, peel off the skin, and mash the flesh. Wash, dry, and toast the seeds for snacking. Many years ago on a call-in radio cooking show about pumpkins and squash, a man called to say that the best pumpkins for pie were cheese pumpkins. Shaped like a wheel of cheese, these hard-to-find pumpkins are squat and brownish and contain less moisture than other pumpkins, making them less likely to water down in a pie. If you can't find cheese pumpkins, drain pumpkin or squash puree in a sieve for an hour before using.

•

Ad in the *Rutland Herald*, October 1, 1996:

Apples, "Face Pumpkins," Home-baked Pies,
Sweet Cider, Pumpkins & Gourds
OPEN 7 DAYS A WEEK
Burnham Hollow Country Store

Almond Pumpkin Cake

When you bake a cake in a Bundt pan, it always looks so festive and it serves at least twelve. This nutty pumpkin cake keeps well and actually improves in flavor after a day or two. Although I rarely sift, it is a good idea when using cake flour because it clumps. If you don't want to make the glaze, just sprinkle the cooled cake with confectioners' sugar.

3 cups cake flour
2 teaspoons baking powder
1 teaspoon baking soda
¼ teaspoon salt
2 cups finely chopped almonds, skins on
2 cups granulated sugar
1 cup (2 sticks) unsalted butter, melted
3 large eggs
1 teaspoon pure vanilla extract
⅛ teaspoon pure almond extract
2 cups fresh or canned pumpkin puree

ALMOND CREAM GLAZE
½ cup confectioners' sugar
¼ cup heavy cream
⅛ teaspoon pure almond extract

Preheat the oven to 350°F. Grease and flour a 10-inch Bundt pan, tapping out any excess flour. Sift together the flour, baking powder and soda, and salt in a medium-size bowl and toss with the nuts. In a large bowl, cream together the sugar, butter, eggs, and extracts together with an electric mixer on high speed until thick. Mix in the pumpkin on low speed and gradually stir in the flour mixture just until the flour is moistened.

Scrape the batter into the pan and bake until a toothpick inserted into the center of the cake comes out clean, about 1¼ hours. Remove the pan to a rack and cool completely. Loosen the edges of the cake with a knife and invert onto a serving plate.

Mix together the glaze ingredients in a small bowl until smooth and drizzle over the cake. The glaze will remain moist, so take care if wrapping the cake when storing.

Spicy Molasses and Pumpkin Cake

MAKES ONE 9 × 13-INCH CAKE

Dark and aromatic, this moist cake is a type of gingerbread, the old but new cake that everyone loves. To frost it or not is up to you. Sometimes I make a lemon sauce to serve atop the squares of cakes, and other times I simply whip some cream to serve alongside. Serve this cake slightly warm on a day when you have been raking the leaves and putting the garden to bed for the winter.

½ cup (1 stick) unsalted butter, at room temperature

¾ cup sugar

3 large eggs

1 cup fresh or canned pumpkin puree

½ cup unsulfured dark molasses

3 cups all-purpose flour

1½ teaspoons baking soda

1½ teaspoons ground cinnamon

2 teaspoons ground ginger

¼ teaspoon ground cloves

½ teaspoon salt

½ cup hot water

continued

Preheat the oven to 350°F. Grease a 9 × 13-inch baking pan. In a large bowl, cream together the butter and sugar with an electric mixer on high speed until light and fluffy. Beat in the eggs, one at a time, scraping down the sides of the bowl after each addition. Mix in the pumpkin and molasses on low speed; the mixture will look curdled. In a small bowl, stir together the flour, baking soda, spices, and salt. With the mixer on low speed, mix in the flour mixture. Mix in the water. Continue to mix on low speed until the batter is smooth, about 2 minutes.

Spread the batter evenly in the pan and bake until a toothpick inserted into the center of the cake comes out clean, 40 to 50 minutes. Cool on a rack until just warm before cutting and serving.

Pumpkin Ginger Pie

Most suppers in the fall will have a pumpkin pie as one of the choices for dessert. Those of you who have never made a pie using fresh pumpkin will be happily surprised at its delicate texture and flavor. Any of the winter squashes can be used in the recipes because the pumpkin season is short and the squashes are good winter keepers. I always pre-bake the crust for any custard pie to avoid a soggy bottom.

FOR THE PASTRY

1 cup all-purpose flour

1 teaspoon sugar

½ teaspoon salt

2 tablespoons cold unsalted butter, cut into pieces

3 tablespoons cold vegetable shortening

3 tablespoons cold water

FOR THE FILLING

2 large eggs

⅓ cup sugar

1 teaspoon pure vanilla extract

1½ cups fresh pumpkin or squash puree

½ cup milk

¼ cup heavy cream

1 teaspoon peeled and grated fresh ginger

To make the dough, combine the flour, sugar, and salt in a small bowl. Add the butter and shortening and cut into the flour using a pastry blender or rub it in with your fingers until the mixture looks like oatmeal. Stir in the water with a fork until a dough forms, adding more water if needed. Gather the dough into a ball, dust with flour, cover with plastic wrap or waxed paper, and chill for at least 1 hour.

Preheat the oven to 400°F. To assemble, roll out the dough on a lightly floured worktable with a floured rolling pin into an 11-inch circle. Drape it over the rolling pin, fit it into a 9-inch pie plate, and crimp the edges. Line the dough with aluminum foil and cover with rice or dried beans. Bake until the edges are set, about 10 minutes, then carefully remove the foil and rice or beans, prick the dough all over with a fork, and bake until the crust is barely colored, 8 to 10 minutes more. Remove from the oven.

To make the filling, whisk together the eggs, sugar, and vanilla in a medium-size bowl until blended. Whisk in the remaining ingredients until smooth and pour into the pie crust. Bake for 10 minutes, reduce the oven temperature to 350°F, and bake until the filling is set, 25 to 30 minutes longer. The center may still be soft but it will firm up as it cools. Cool completely on a rack before serving.

COUNTRY TIPS AND TALES

The rice or beans used for prebaked pie crusts may be used again and again. Store the cooled rice or beans in the cupboard in a covered container marked PIE RICE/BEANS.

Lattice-Topped Squash and Apple Pie

Every fall at Spring Lake Ranch, the therapeutic community where I worked for six years, we would celebrate the end of the garden season with a big harvest supper. The meal featured all of the foods grown on the ranch, and we always served those enormous Hubbard squashes, all knobby and blue. This pie combines squash and apples in a flavorful, old-fashioned pie.

FOR THE PASTRY

2 cups all-purpose flour

1 tablespoon sugar

1 teaspoon salt

¼ cup (½ stick) cold unsalted butter, cut into pieces

1 cup cold vegetable shortening

⅓ cup cold water

FOR THE FILLING

1 pound butternut squash

1 pound apples, such as Cortland or Northern Spy, peeled, cored, and
     coarsely grated

⅔ cup plus 1 tablespoon sugar

2 tablespoons cornstarch

½ teaspoon ground cinnamon

¼ teaspoon freshly grated nutmeg

2 tablespoons unsalted butter, melted

1 teaspoon fresh lemon juice

1 tablespoon milk

To make the dough, stir the flour, sugar, and salt together in a medium-size bowl. Cut in the butter and shortening with a pastry blender or rub it in with your fingers until the mixture looks like oatmeal. Stir in the water with a fork until a dough forms, adding more water if needed. Gather the dough into a disk, dust with flour, cover with plastic wrap or waxed paper, and chill for at least 1 hour.

To make the filling, cut the skin off the squash with a sharp knife and scoop out the seeds. Coarsely grate the squash and place the squash and the apples in a large bowl. Mix the ⅔ cup sugar, the cornstarch, cinnamon, and nutmeg together and toss with the squash and apples. Add the butter and lemon juice and toss again.

Preheat the oven to 450°F. To assemble, divide the dough in half and roll out on a lightly floured worktable with a floured rolling pin into an 11-inch circle. Drape over the rolling pin, fit the dough into a 9-inch pie plate and spoon in the filling. Lightly flour the surface, roll out the remaining dough, and cut into ten ½-inch-wide strips. Arrange the strips over the filling, weaving them in and out for a lattice pattern. Trim the pastry to a 1-inch overhang and decoratively crimp the edges with a fork. Brush the lattice with the milk and sprinkle with the remaining tablespoon of sugar.

Bake the pie for 15 minutes, reduce the temperature to 350°F, and bake until the crust is browned and the filling is tender when pierced with a fork, about 30 minutes. Cool completely on a rack before serving.

COUNTY TIPS AND TALES

One late summer morning, my mother-in-law discovered that a woodchuck had taken one bite out of every butternut squash in the garden. This, of course, ruined the crop for winter storage. She took her revenge!

Butternut Squash Pudding

MAKES 6 TO 8 SERVINGS

Our foliage season can be glorious, with brilliantly clear days that make the leaves radiate with color. A warm squash pudding is the perfect ending to a supper with friends on an autumn weekend. Puddings like this one were more common in the past when calorie watching was not such a priority.

4 large eggs plus 3 large egg yolks

½ cup pure dark amber or grade B maple syrup

2 cups butternut squash puree, drained ½ hour in a fine-meshed sieve

2 cups heavy cream

1 teaspoon pure vanilla extract

Preheat the oven to 350°F. Whisk together the whole eggs, yolks, and maple syrup in a large bowl until well blended. Whisk in the squash, cream, and vanilla. Pour into an ungreased 2-quart casserole. Place the casserole in a larger baking pan and set the pan on the center oven rack. Carefully add enough hot water to the baking pan to come halfway up the casserole. Bake until the pudding is set and a knife inserted in the center comes out clean, 30 to 40 minutes. Remove the casserole from the water and cool on a rack until warm before serving.

COUNTRY TIPS AND TALES

Notice in the *Rutland Herald*, September 17, 1996:

Pumpkin Day
Woodstock
Learn about the many uses of pumpkin through
a variety of activities and take home your own
Jack-Be-Little miniature pumpkin, harvest activities
and horse drawn wagon rides, begins at 10 A.M.
Billings Farm and Museum

Flan de Calabaza

MAKES 6 TO 8 SERVINGS

Cati Larkin was born in Manati, Puerto Rico, and lived in San Juan for many years. When her husband found a teaching job at a local college she moved the family to Clarendon, Vermont. After six years, she has become accustomed to wearing many layers of clothing and says that Vermont "grows on you." Cati loves to cook and share her native dishes, especially this delicious pumpkin flan, which seems very suitable to New England fare. The flan needs to be made the day before serving to firm up for easier slicing, so plan ahead.

2 cups sugar

¼ cup water

2 cups milk

2 teaspoons spiced rum or dark rum

Pinch of salt

6 large eggs

2 cups fresh or canned pumpkin puree

½ cup (1 stick) unsalted butter, melted

⅔ cup all-purpose flour

Preheat the oven to 350°F. Place 1 cup of the sugar in a small, heavy-bottomed pot with the water and cook over medium heat, stirring to dissolve the sugar. Cook until the caramel turns a deep amber color, 5 to 10 minutes. Immediately pour the caramel into an ungreased 8-cup casserole or deep cake pan and swirl the pan until the caramel coats the dish or pan bottom. Let cool.

Heat the milk, rum, and salt together in a saucepan over medium heat until hot. In a large bowl, whisk together the eggs and the remaining sugar until blended, and very gradually whisk in the hot milk. Stir, trying not to create bubbles, until the sugar dissolves. Mix together the pumpkin, butter, and flour in another large bowl and stir in the egg-milk mixture. Pour into the casserole.

Place the casserole in a larger baking pan on the center rack of the oven. Carefully fill the outer pan with enough hot water to come two thirds of the way up the sides of the casserole. Bake until a knife inserted in the center comes out clean, about 1¼ hours. Remove the casserole from the water to cool on a rack. Cover the casserole with plastic wrap and refrigerate overnight.

To unmold, run a knife around the edges and invert the flan into a deep serving dish large enough to hold the caramel syrup.

COUNTRY TIPS AND TALES

Better a little pumpkin in your hand
than a big one in the field.
—Talmud: Sukkoh, 566

Maple Cup Custards

MAKES 8 SERVINGS

Cup custards are truly comfort foods, smooth and silky. The same mixture poured over bread and baked makes a delicious bread pudding. For the best maple flavor, use maple sugar or grade B syrup. Save the fancy stuff for pancakes.

    4 large eggs plus 4 large yolks
    1 cup firmly packed pure maple sugar
    3 cups milk
    1 cup heavy cream
    1 teaspoon pure vanilla extract

Preheat the oven to 350°F. Whisk together the eggs, yolks, and sugar in a medium-size bowl until the sugar is dissolved. Whisk in the milk, cream, and vanilla. Pour into 8 custard cups or other ovenproof baking cups and place them in a large baking dish on the center rack. Carefully pour hot water into the baking pan so that it comes halfway up the custard cups. Bake until the custards are set and a knife inserted in the center comes out clean, 40 to 45 minutes. Remove the cups from the water and cool on a rack. Refrigerate if not serving right away.

COUNTRY TIPS AND TALES

Occasionally maple syrup starts to ferment and taste "off." Simply add a tablespoon of cream to the syrup, bring it to a boil in a nonreactive saucepan, and skim off any foam that rises. Cool and refrigerate.

Trish's Maple Cream Fudge

Trish Norton and husband, Art Krueger, share a philosophy of living a low-impact life on this earth. They use solar, wind, and wood power on their Cuttingsville farmstead. With their three little girls, they have a large garden, do lots of canning, and make maple syrup and fudge. Trish says occasionally the sugar content in a particular batch of syrup isn't heavy enough to let the fudge set up for cutting. She suggests rolling pieces of such fudge into balls for "truffles" or heating the fudge with some water for an ice cream sauce. As Trish was explaining the quick timing of this fudge recipe to me, nine-year-old Rosie sighed, "It always seems so long to me when I'm waiting to lick the spoon."

1 quart pure dark amber or grade B maple syrup
¼ cup (½ stick) unsalted butter
Pinch of salt
1 cup heavy cream
1 cup coarsely chopped walnuts

Butter an 8-inch-square cake pan. In a large heavy-bottomed pan, cook the syrup with the butter, salt, and cream over medium heat until the temperature reaches 236°F on a candy thermometer. To keep the fudge from becoming gritty, do not stir the mixture until it cools to 120°F, and beat with a wooden spoon or paddle until the mixture begins to stiffen. It will look whiter and start to stiffen in about 3 minutes. Add the walnuts and quickly spread the mixture evenly in the pan. Cool for several hours. Invert the pan onto a cutting board, remove the pan, and cut into squares with a long sharp knife.

Wrap individual pieces in plastic and store in the refrigerator, as the creamy texture starts to change if kept at room temperature.

Maple Walnut Sundaes

MAKES 4 SERVINGS

Many years ago, my friend Nancy and I would eat "wet" walnut sundaes with coffee ice cream at the corner store near our school. It still is one of my favorite combinations of flavors, made better by toasting the walnuts and using pure maple syrup. If you have some tall parfait glasses stuck away in your china closet, use them for this treat. My husband asks, "Where's the whipped cream?" but I say, enough's enough!

1 cup coarsely chopped walnuts
1 pint coffee ice cream
½ cup pure dark amber or grade B maple syrup

Preheat the oven to 350°F. Spread the walnuts on a cookie sheet and toast for 7 to 9 minutes. Cool. Remove the ice cream from the freezer and let it soften enough so it spoons easily. Mix the nuts with the syrup and spoon a bit into each parfait glass. Spoon in some ice cream, more nuts and syrup, ice cream, and a final topping of the nuts and syrup.

Serve immediately or cover with plastic wrap and freeze for 1 day. Remove from the freezer and let sit in the refrigerator for 1 hour before serving.

COUNTRY TIPS AND TALES

Some ways of measuring from the past . . .

The bigth of a walnut,
Enough to lie on a pen knife's point,
The weight of a shilling,
As big as a haselnut,
The bigth of a Turkey's egg,
A bunch of pretty herbs.
—*Green Mountain Whittlin's*

Ragamuffins

When there isn't time to make a yeast dough and you need a fast dessert, make these meltingly good biscuits. I found a similar recipe in an old copy of *Green Mountain Whittlin's* and it is reminiscent of jam roll-ups. Why these are called ragamuffins is unknown, for the name pertains to a dirty or untidily dressed child!

FOR THE DOUGH

2 cups all-purpose flour

4 teaspoons baking powder

½ teaspoon salt

3 tablespoons cold vegetable shortening

1 tablespoon cold unsalted butter

⅔ cup milk

FOR THE FILLING

¼ cup (½ stick) unsalted butter, at room temperature

1 cup firmly packed maple sugar or light brown sugar

Preheat the oven to 400°F. Line a cookie sheet with parchment paper. To make the dough, stir together the flour, baking powder, and salt in a medium-size bowl. Cut in the shortening and butter with a pastry blender or rub it in with your fingers until the mixture resemble oatmeal. Stir in the milk with a fork just until a soft dough forms. Knead the dough 7 to 8 times on a lightly floured worktable and roll out with a floured rolling pin into a 10 × 12-inch rectangle about ⅓ inch thick.

For the filling, carefully spread the softened butter over the surface of the dough and evenly sprinkle on the maple sugar. Roll up the dough from the long end like a jelly roll and pinch the seam shut. With a sharp, floured knife, cut the roll into 16 pieces. Place the pieces cut side down on a cookie sheet about 2 inches apart. Bake until golden brown, 18 to 20 minutes. Serve warm.

Maple-Nut Sticky Buns

MAKES 12 BUNS

If there is anyone who can resist sticky buns, I haven't yet met that person. Rob McKain, the co-chef at Spring Lake Ranch, makes his sticky buns with a light, buttery dough and pecans. Make a double batch of sticky buns and freeze a pan of unbaked buns for another day, then defrost, let rise in the pan, and bake.

FOR THE DOUGH

2 tablespoons (2 envelopes) dry yeast

1 tablespoon pure maple syrup

1½ cups warm buttermilk (about 115° F)

6 to 7 cups all-purpose flour

2 teaspoons salt

2 large eggs

2 tablespoons unsalted butter, melted

FOR THE FILLING

2 tablespoons unsalted butter, melted

½ cup finely chopped pecans or walnuts

¼ cup firmly packed maple sugar or light brown sugar

1 teaspoon ground cinnamon

FOR THE TOPPING

1 cup pure dark amber or grade B maple syrup

3 tablespoons unsalted butter, melted

To make the dough, place the yeast, maple syrup, and ½ cup of the buttermilk in the bowl of an electric mixer fitted with a dough hook and stir to combine. Let sit 5 minutes, until bubbly. If it doesn't bubble, that means the yeast is no longer active and must be replaced. Mix in 5 cups of the flour, the salt, eggs, butter, and the remaining buttermilk and knead with the machine on slow speed. Add the remaining cup flour until a dough forms and cleans the sides of the bowl. The dough should be soft but not sticky and feel elastic to the touch.

If making by hand, stir the flour, salt, eggs, butter, and the remaining buttermilk into the yeast mixture with a wooden spoon, turn the dough out onto a well-floured worktable and knead, adding more flour until the dough cleans the table, is soft but not sticky, and feels elastic to the touch, 8 to 10 minutes.

Place the dough in a large bowl. Sprinkle it with flour, cover the bowl with a clean kitchen towel, and let rise in a warm draft-free place until doubled, about 1 hour.

Punch the air out of the dough and turn it onto a floured worktable. Roll the dough into a 12 × 16-inch rectangle about ½ inch thick. Brush the dough with the melted butter. Mix the nuts, maple sugar, and cinnamon together in a small bowl and sprinkle over the dough. Roll up the dough from the short end like a jelly roll and pinch the seam tightly shut. With a sharp floured knife, cut the roll into 12 buns. Spread the syrup and butter for the topping in a 9 × 13-inch baking pan and place the buns cut side down 1 inch apart on the syrup. Cover with the kitchen towel and let rise until the dough fills the pan, about 45 minutes.

Preheat the oven to 375°F. Bake until the buns are golden brown, about 40 minutes. Remove the pan from the oven and let cool 10 minutes. Loosen the edges with a knife and invert onto a serving platter.

Grandpère

MAKES 6 TO 8 SERVINGS

Lorraine Kimble, who now lives in Brandon, grew up in a French-speaking community in southern Maine. She remembers grating a block of maple sugar for her mother to make this dessert. She thinks it got its name from the fact that it was grandpère's (grandfather's) favorite dessert. I also found a similar recipe for maple syrup dumplings in *Out of Old Nova Scotia Kitchens* by Marie Nightingale.

2 cups all-purpose flour

2 teaspoons baking powder

½ teaspoon baking soda

½ teaspoon salt

2 tablespoons cold unsalted butter, cut into pieces

¾ cup buttermilk

2 cups pure dark amber or grade B maple syrup

2 cups water

Plain yogurt, sour cream, or crème fraîche (page 2)

continued

Stir together the flour, baking powder and soda, and salt in a medium-size bowl. Cut in the butter with a pastry blender or rub it in with your fingers until the mixture resembles oatmeal. Stir in the buttermilk just until the flour mixture is moistened.

Heat the syrup and water together in a 10-inch skillet over medium heat until boiling. Drop heaping tablespoons of the batter into the syrup, leaving spaces for the dumplings to expand. Cover the skillet, reduce the heat to low, and simmer until the dumplings are dry to the touch, about 20 minutes. Spoon into a serving dish and serve warm with yogurt or the topping of your choice.

COUNTRY TIPS AND TALES

The dumplings in a dream are not dumplings, but dreams.
—*Leo Rosten's Treasury of Jewish Quotations*

Cinnamon Cake with Maple Cream Frosting

MAKES ONE 9-INCH LAYER CAKE

Make this tender cake to celebrate someone special, for a birthday or an anniversary. The frosting is an Italian meringue of hot syrup beaten into whipped egg whites. You will need a candy thermometer for this. Remember, the more you cream the butter and sugar, the better texture the cake will have.

FOR THE CAKE

2 cups cake flour

2 teaspoons ground cinnamon

2 teaspoons baking powder

½ teaspoon baking soda

¼ teaspoon salt

⅛ teaspoon ground cloves

½ cup (1 stick) unsalted butter, at room temperature

1 cup firmly packed light brown sugar

2 large eggs

1 cup buttermilk

FOR THE FROSTING

¾ cup pure dark amber or grade B maple syrup

3 large egg whites

Pinch of salt

Preheat the oven to 350°F. Grease and line the bottoms of two 9-inch cake pans with parchment or waxed paper. To make the cake, sift the flour, cinnamon, baking powder and soda, salt, and cloves together in a medium-size bowl. In a large bowl, cream together the butter and sugar with an electric mixer on high speed until very light and fluffy. Beat in the eggs, one at a time, scraping down the sides of the bowl after each addition. On low speed, mix in the flour mixture alternately with the buttermilk. Spread the batter evenly in the pans. Bake until the cakes are golden brown and a toothpick inserted in the center of each cake comes out clean, 25 to 30 minutes.

Cool on a rack for 20 minutes. Loosen the edges of the cakes with a knife and invert onto racks to finish cooling. Remove the pans and peel off the paper.

To make the frosting, heat the syrup in a heavy-bottomed saucepan until it reaches 230°F on a candy thermometer. Whip together the egg whites and salt in a large bowl with an electric mixer on medium speed until soft peaks form. When the syrup reaches 238°F, with the mixer on medium speed, pour a steady stream of the syrup down the side of the bowl. The meringue will expand as it absorbs the syrup. Continue to whip the meringue until it cools, about 5 minutes.

To assemble, place one cake layer on a 9-inch circle of cardboard. Spread about 1½ cups of the frosting on this layer. Place the second layer bottom side up on the first and cover the sides and top with the remaining frosting. Place the cake on a serving plate.

> ### COUNTRY TIPS AND TALES
>
> Meringue frosting will stay glossy only for a day or two and then it gets stippled looking, though it still tastes good.

Dark Syrup Vinegar Cake with Cardamom Sauce

MAKES ONE 9-INCH-SQUARE CAKE

The darkest maple syrup is not for retail sale. It is reserved for commercial producers who dilute the heavy maple with other sugar syrups to get maple-flavored syrups. The smart farmer, though, reserves some of this syrup for personal use, as the maple flavor is intense. If you can, sweet-talk a maple grower into giving you some bottom-of-the-barrel stuff, or use grade B syrup to make this old-fashioned cake. The cardamom sauce comes from a Swedish friend who uses this spice to great effect.

FOR THE CAKE

½ cup (1 stick) unsalted butter, at room temperature

½ cup sugar

1 large egg

1 cup pure maple syrup

¼ cup cider vinegar

1 teaspoon pure vanilla extract

2 cups all-purpose flour

1 teaspoon baking soda

½ teaspoon salt

½ cup hot water

FOR THE SAUCE

½ cup sour cream

¼ cup plain yogurt

3 tablespoons sugar

¼ teaspoon ground cardamom

Preheat the oven to 350°F. Grease a 9-inch-square baking pan. To make the cake, in a large bowl, cream together the butter and sugar with an electric mixer on high speed until light and fluffy. Reduce the speed to low and stir in the egg, syrup, vinegar, and vanilla until blended. Stir together the flour, baking soda, and salt in a small bowl and add to the butter mixture, mixing for 2 minutes. Add the hot water and mix until the batter is smooth, about 1 minute longer. Scrape into the pan and bake until a toothpick inserted into the center of the cake comes out clean, about 35 minutes. Cool on a rack and serve from the pan.

To make the sauce, stir the sauce ingredients together in a bowl. The cardamom flavor becomes more pronounced if the sauce rests for 1 hour before serving.

Cranberry Maple Tart

MAKES ONE 9-INCH TART

You will need a 9-inch removable-bottom tart pan for this crunchy, sweet, and tangy tart. Serve small slices with barely sweetened whipped cream on the side. It is New England's answer to pecan pie and anyone who has eaten it always asks for the recipe.

FOR THE PASTRY

1 cup all-purpose flour

1 teaspoon sugar

½ teaspoon salt

2 tablespoons cold unsalted butter, cut into pieces

1 tablespoon cold vegetable shortening

3 tablespoons cold water

FOR THE FILLING

3 large eggs

½ cup firmly packed dark brown sugar

¾ cup pure dark amber or grade B maple syrup

¼ cup (½ stick) unsalted butter, melted

1 cup coarsely chopped fresh cranberries

1 cup coarsely chopped walnuts

To make the dough, stir together the flour, sugar, and salt in a medium-size bowl. Cut in the butter and shortening with a pastry blender or rub it in with your fingers until the mixture resembles oatmeal. Stir in the water with a fork until the dough forms a ball, adding more water if needed. Gather the dough into a ball, dust with flour, cover with plastic wrap or waxed paper, and chill for at least 1 hour.

Preheat the oven to 425°F. To assemble, roll out the dough with a floured rolling pin on a lightly floured worktable into an 11-inch circle, drape it over the rolling pin, and fit it in the tart pan. Trim any overhanging dough to a ½-inch edge and fold it over to make a double layer around the edge, pushing the dough up ¼ inch above the tart rim.

Place the eggs in a medium-size bowl and whisk until foamy. Beat in the sugar, syrup, and butter until well combined. Stir in the cranberries and walnuts. Pour into the tart pan and bake for 15 minutes. Reduce the oven temperature to 350°F and bake until the filling is puffed and lightly browned, about 25 minutes. Cool completely on a rack. Gently push the bottom of the tart pan up to remove the sides. Place the tart on a serving plate, leaving the tart pan bottom in place to support the crust.

COUNTRY TIPS AND TALES

Promises and pie-crusts are made to be broken.
—Jonathan Swift (1667—1745), *Polite Conversation*

Maple Buttermilk Pie

MAKES ONE 9-INCH PIE

Buttermilk is what remains from cream after churning it into butter. When cooked in a pie, it becomes almost like cheesecake and is sure to please. Occasionally there will be a pie auction as a charity event, and the best-looking pies bring in the money. Our renowned auctioneer, Bus Mars, calls out in his unique cadence, selling the pie to the highest bidder. His good-natured crowd heckling often gets you buying a pie you made yourself!

1 cup all-purpose flour

1 teaspoon sugar

½ teaspoon salt

2 tablespoons cold unsalted butter, cut into pieces

3 tablespoons cold vegetable shortening

3 tablespoons cold water

FOR THE FILLING

3 large eggs plus 3 large egg yolks

⅔ cup pure dark amber or grade B maple syrup

1 teaspoon pure vanilla extract

¼ teaspoon salt

2 cups buttermilk

To make the dough, stir together the flour, sugar, and salt in a small bowl. Cut in the butter and shortening with a pastry blender or rub it in with your fingers until the mixture resembles oatmeal. Stir in the water with a fork until the dough forms, adding more water if needed. Gather the dough into a ball, dust with flour, cover with plastic wrap or waxed paper, and chill for at least 1 hour.

Preheat the oven to 400°F. Roll out the dough with a floured rolling pin on a lightly floured worktable into an 11-inch circle. Drape it over the rolling pin, fit it into a 9-inch pie plate, and crimp the edges with a fork. Line the dough with aluminum foil and fill with rice or dried beans. Bake until the edges are set, about 10 minutes, then carefully remove the foil and rice or beans, prick the dough all over with a fork, and bake until the crust is barely colored, 8 to 10 minutes more. Remove from the oven. Reduce the oven temperature to 350°F.

Beat together the whole eggs and yolks in a medium-size bowl until frothy. Whisk in the maple syrup, vanilla, and salt until well combined. Stir in the buttermilk and pour the mixture into the pie crust. Bake until the custard is set but the center is still soft, about 40 minutes. Cool on a rack. Refrigerate if not serving within 2 hours.

Chocolate Desserts

ASK MOST PEOPLE WHAT their favorite flavor is and they will say "chocolate." Usually the first things anyone learns to bake are chocolate chip cookies and brownies. In fact, that is as far as some people get! You will invariably find these treats at community bake sales, and at the suppers a chocolate pie will be the first to disappear.

In our family, there are some serious chocolate lovers. My son-in-law comes from an entire family of chocolate eaters. His Christmas presents this year ran strictly on a one-note theme—chocolate. My sister, Jessica Reisman, owns a bakery in Seattle where she sells several delicious cookies based on this confection. You can always count on her to bring a chocolate treat when she's invited for supper.

Once I had to judge a chocolate contest for a national magazine. After reading through 2,500 entries, I picked out seventy of the most unusual and interesting. Then I cooked and sampled all seventy to find the five best recipes, which won the contest. It was a tough assignment, and I couldn't look at or eat chocolate for at least a year.

There is good chocolate and there is great chocolate. Vermont has become a chocolate lover's dream. There are several fine chocolate candy manufacturers, a cocoa company, and, of course, who hasn't tried Ben & Jerry's New York Super Fudge Chunk ice cream? Even the supermarkets carry chocolate chips in a profusion of flavors.

Whenever you are in doubt over which dessert to make for supper, make it chocolate. Many chocolate recipes became heirlooms because the cook liked to eat what she made.

Chocolate Shortbread

These melt-in-your-mouth cookies have a deep chocolate flavor that comes from Dutch-processed cocoa. I use the Droste or the Callebaut brand, which gives a much richer taste than Hershey's. The cookies get better after a day or two because the flavor develops. Too fragile to travel, these cookies are best stored in a tightly covered container with waxed paper between the layers.

2 cups all-purpose flour
1¼ cups confectioners' sugar
½ cup unsweetened cocoa powder
1½ cups (3 sticks) unsalted butter, at room temperature

Sift together the flour, 1 cup of the sugar, and the cocoa in a medium-size bowl. Cream the butter and the flour mixture with a wooden spoon until the dough is smooth. Alternatively, use an electric mixer on low speed. Scrape the dough into an ungreased 15 × 11-inch jelly roll pan and press evenly in the pan with floured fingertips. Refrigerate the dough for 10 minutes.

Preheat the oven to 325°F. Remove the dough from the refrigerator and cut it lengthwise into 4 strips, then cut it crosswise into 8 strips to make 32 rectangles. Cut each rectangle in half diagonally, then prick each triangle twice with a fork. Bake until the top of the shortbread feels dry, about 20 minutes. Remove the pan to a rack, cool for 5 minutes, and recut the cookies while warm. When completely cool, sprinkle with the remaining ¼ cup confectioners' sugar.

COUNTRY TIPS AND TALES

Shortbread cookies were not everyday fare, but reserved for weddings, christenings, or when important guests came to call. A tea party in Scotland was known as a "cooky-shine."

Almond Coconut
Chocolate Kisses

MAKES ABOUT 4 DOZEN COOKIES

While remembering cookies, my sister reminded me of our child-hood favorite. Mom made chewy meringues from the recipe on the cornflake box and we adored them. I added chocolate, skipped the cereal, and came up with a new cookie-candy that is scrumptious.

8 ounces whole almonds, skins on
4 large egg whites
Pinch of salt
¾ cup sugar
8 ounces bittersweet chocolate, chopped
2 cups unsweetened shredded coconut

Preheat the oven to 350°F. Place the almonds on a cookie sheet and toast in the center of the oven until lightly brown, 7 to 9 minutes. Cool and chop very coarsely. Reduce the oven temperature to 250°F.

Lightly grease 2 cookie sheets. In a large bowl, beat the egg whites and salt with an electric mixer on medium speed until soft peaks form. Gradually beat in the sugar until a stiff meringue forms. Fold in the nuts, chocolate, and coconut. Drop rounded tablespoons about 1 inch apart on the cookie sheets. Bake until the cookies feel dry to the touch, about 45 minutes. Remove from the oven and cool completely on the cookie sheets. Store in a tightly covered container.

COUNTRY TIPS AND TALES

Bachelor's fare: bread and cheese, and kisses
—Jonathan Swift (1667—1745), *Polite Conversation*

Old-fashioned Chocolate Jumbles

MAKES 8 DOZEN 3-INCH COOKIES

Jeannette Kling, my sister-in-law, shares her husband's grand-mother's chocolate jumble cookie recipe, which has been in the family for over one hundred years and reflects the Klings' German heritage. They have been dairy farmers for more than four generations and enjoy this mildly spiced chocolate cookie that goes great with a glass of milk.

This is a good dough for making holiday cookies and gingerbread people. You can ice them with a simple white confectioners' sugar icing or a thin chocolate icing and decorate with colored sprinkles or sugars, cinnamon candies, or silver dragees.

The dough needs overnight chilling to allow for easier rolling; this also allows the flavors to mellow. Watch them carefully during baking—dough containing molasses and chocolate burns easily.

THE COOKIES

5 cups all-purpose flour

¾ cup Dutch-processed unsweetened cocoa powder

2 teaspoons baking soda

1 teaspoon ground cinnamon

1 teaspoon ground cloves

1 cup granulated sugar

1 cup (2 sticks) unsalted butter, at room temperature

1 large egg

1 cup unsulfured dark molasses

1 tablespoon cider vinegar

1 tablespoon pure vanilla extract

¾ cup hot strong coffee

FOR THE ICING

1½ cups sifted confectioners' sugar

3 tablespoons heavy cream

1 teaspoon pure vanilla extract

continued

Sift together the flour, cocoa, baking soda, and spices in a large bowl. In another large bowl, cream together the sugar and butter with an electric mixer on high speed until light and fluffy. Beat in the egg and molasses and scrape down the sides of the bowl. Reduce to low speed and stir in the vinegar, vanilla, and coffee. Stir in the flour mixture until the flour is just moistened. Do not overmix. Chill the dough overnight.

Preheat the oven to 375°F. Lightly grease cookie sheets. Divide the dough and roll out one quarter of the cookie dough with a floured rolling pin on a lightly floured work-table to ¼ inch thick. Keep the remaining dough in the refrigerator until you are ready to use it. Reroll cookie scraps. These cookies are traditionally cut with a doughnut cutter, but any shape is fine. Place the cookies 1 inch apart on cookie sheets and bake 8 to 10 minutes. Cool completely on a rack.

In a medium-size bowl, mix together the icing ingredients together until smooth and ice the cookies when they are cool. Store in a tightly covered container with waxed paper between the layers of cookies.

COUNTRY TIPS AND TALES

Ovens have hot spots, so it is wise to rotate cookie sheets halfway through baking. This ensures evenly baked cookies.

Helen's Chocolate Rugelach

MAKES 64 RUGELACH

Helen Snyder, from Florence, Vermont, is full of energy and enthusiasm for whatever comes her way. She bakes these fabulous little pastries for her son, Andy, to sell at his farm stand. We brought her rugelach to a friend's wedding and they were devoured in moments.

FOR THE PASTRY

1 cup (2 sticks) unsalted butter, at room temperature

One 8-ounce package cream cheese, at room temperature

¼ cup sugar

½ teaspoon salt

2 cups all-purpose flour

FOR THE FILLING

8 ounces bittersweet chocolate, finely chopped

1¼ cups finely chopped pecans

½ cup sugar

1 tablespoon ground cinnamon

Egg wash made from 1 large egg beaten with 1 tablespoon water

To make the pastry, cream together the butter, cream cheese, sugar, and salt in a large bowl with an electric mixer on low speed. Gradually add the flour until blended. Divide the dough into 4 balls, dust with flour, and cover with plastic wrap or waxed paper. Chill for at least 1 hour.

Preheat the oven to 375°F. Grease 2 cookie sheets. To make the filling, stir together the chocolate, pecans, sugar, and cinnamon in a small bowl. On a lightly floured worktable, roll out one ball of the dough with a floured rolling pin into a 12-inch circle. Brush the dough with the egg wash. Sprinkle evenly with one quarter of the filling. Cut the circle into 16 triangles with a long, sharp knife. Roll each triangle up firmly from the flat end to the point. Place each rugelach point down on a cookie sheet and repeat with the remaining dough and filling. Brush the tops of the rugelach with egg wash.

Bake until golden brown, 15 to 20 minutes. Immediately remove the rugelach to a rack to cool. Rugelach are at their best when fresh and will freeze beautifully if frozen unbaked. Thaw and bake as directed.

COUNTRY TIPS AND TALES

Do not freeze cookie dough for more than 3 months

Hot Chocolate Pudding
with Custard Sauce

MAKES 4 TO 6 SERVINGS

Adapted from an old family cookbook found on a dusty shelf in a used bookstore, this recipe is typical of hot baked puddings in English cooking. Served with a silky custard sauce, it is elegant, yet homey, and is a welcome treat on a cold winter night. It can also be served warm or even cold. When cold, the pudding loses its delicate quality, yet it still tastes fine.

FOR THE CUSTARD SAUCE

2 cups milk

4 large egg yolks

¼ cup sugar

1 teaspoon pure vanilla extract

FOR THE PUDDING

¼ cup (½ stick) unsalted butter, at room temperature

½ cup sugar

1 large egg

2 squares (2 ounces) unsweetened chocolate, melted

½ cup milk

½ cup all-purpose flour

1 teaspoon baking powder

To make the custard sauce, scald the milk in a 1½-quart heavy-bottomed saucepan over medium-low heat. Whisk the egg yolks and sugar together in a medium-size bowl and very gradually whisk in the hot milk. Return the mixture to the saucepan and cook over medium-low heat, stirring constantly with a wooden spoon. Cook just until the mixture coats the back of the spoon. Do not boil or the eggs will scramble. Strain the custard through a fine-meshed sieve into a bowl. Stir in the vanilla and cover the surface with plastic wrap to prevent a skin from forming. Refrigerate the custard sauce until cold.

Preheat the oven to 350°F. Grease an 8-inch glass pie plate or gratin dish. To make the pudding, in a large bowl, cream together the butter, sugar, and egg with an electric mixer on high speed until fluffy. Reduce to low speed and stir in the chocolate, then the milk. Mix the flour with the baking powder in a small bowl, add to the chocolate mixture, and stir to combine.

Pour into the pie plate and bake until puffed, about 20 minutes. Cool for 10 minutes. Serve the pudding hot with the chilled custard sauce.

COUNTRY TIPS AND TALES

Chocolate doesn't like high heat, so when melting it, use a heavy-bottomed saucepan on a heat diffuser or melt it in a double boiler over simmering water.

Baked Chocolate Custard

MAKES 4 TO 6 SERVINGS

I have adapted a recipe found in the 1924 *Island Cook Book*, "a collection of approved recipes contributed by the women of Marthas Vineyard." The custard's intense chocolate flavor will please any chocolatephiles invited to your supper table.

1 cup milk

1 cup heavy cream

3 squares (3 ounces) unsweetened chocolate

¾ cup granulated sugar

4 large eggs

1 teaspoon pure vanilla extract

Pinch of salt

FOR THE GARNISH

½ cup heavy cream

1 tablespoon confectioners' sugar

½ teaspoon pure vanilla extract

Preheat the oven to 325°F. Heat the milk, cream, chocolate, and ¼ cup of the granulated sugar in a medium-size saucepan until boiling, stirring, over medium heat. Whisk the remaining ½ cup sugar into the eggs in a large bowl and very gradually stir in the hot chocolate mixture. Pour into a 9-inch nonreactive pie plate or gratin dish. Place the pie plate in a larger baking pan on the center rack of the oven and carefully fill with 1 inch of hot water. Bake until the custard is set but the center still moves, 30 to 40 minutes. Remove the pie plate from the water and cool on a rack. Chill for at least 2 hours before serving.

To make the garnish, whip the cream, sugar, and vanilla with an electric mixer until soft peaks form and spoon dollops on the custard before serving.

COUNTRY TIPS AND TALES

Pipe a pretty lattice of whipped cream on custards and open-faced pies with a pastry bag fitted with a large star tip.

Chocolate Sauerkraut Cupcakes

Many people remember their grandma's kraut cake with delight. When I saw Mary Jirik at the Rutland farmers' market, she gave me her grandmother's recipe. Dale Lincoln, in the farm stand next to hers, overheard us and said his grandmother made one also. I decided to turn the cake into cupcakes for lunch box treats.

FOR THE CUPCAKES

⅔ cup (1 stick plus 2 tablespoons) unsalted butter, at room temperature

1½ cups granulated sugar

3 large eggs

1 teaspoon pure vanilla extract

2¼ cups cake flour

½ cup Dutch-processed unsweetened cocoa powder

1 teaspoon baking powder

1 teaspoon baking soda

½ teaspoon salt

1 cup water

⅔ cup sauerkraut, rinsed, drained, and chopped

FOR THE FROSTING

1½ cups confectioners' sugar

1½ tablespoons Dutch-processed unsweetened cocoa powder

3 tablespoons unsalted butter, at room temperature

3 tablespoons cream cheese, at room temperature

Pinch of salt

1 tablespoon heavy cream

Preheat the oven to 350°F. Line cupcake tins with paper liners. To make the cake, cream together the butter and sugar in a large bowl with an electric mixer on high speed until light and fluffy. Beat in the eggs and vanilla and scrape down the sides of the bowl. Sift together the flour, cocoa, baking powder and soda, and salt in a medium-size bowl and add to the butter mixture on low speed, alternating with the water. Stir in the sauerkraut and spoon into the cupcake tins. Bake until a toothpick inserted into the center of a cupcake comes out clean, about 20 minutes. Cool for 5 minutes, then cool the cupcakes completely on a rack.

To make the frosting, sift together the confectioners' sugar and cocoa in a large bowl. Beat together the butter, cream cheese, salt, and heavy cream with an electric mixer on low speed until blended, increase the speed to high, and beat the frosting until fluffy. Spread the frosting on the cupcakes. Store them in a tightly covered container. They may be frozen for up to 1 month.

COUNTRY TIPS AND TALES

Chocolate was used mainly as a drink until the late 1800s and then only by the wealthy. Mrs. Beeton's 1861 *Book of Household Management* has only one recipe for a chocolate dessert. She also mentions purchasing a box of candies to serve as a seasonal confection.

Zucchini Chocolate-Chip Cake

MAKES ONE 9 × 13-INCH CAKE

Driving past a house, we saw a sign saying "FREE ZUCCHINI" perched on a chair in the front lawn. It made us chuckle. Another poor soul inundated with those large, overgrown zucchini everyone has at the end of the season. This cook thinks this cake is a perfect way to use up that overgrown crop.

1 cup vegetable oil

1¾ cups sugar

2 large eggs

1 teaspoon pure vanilla extract

½ cup buttermilk

2¼ cups all-purpose flour

¼ cup Dutch-processed unsweetened cocoa powder

1 teaspoon baking soda

½ teaspoon baking powder

½ teaspoon ground cinnamon

½ teaspoon salt

¼ teaspoon ground cloves

1½ pounds zucchini, peeled, seeded, and coarsely grated (2 cups)

½ cup chocolate chips

Preheat the oven to 325°F. Grease a 9 × 13-inch baking pan. To make the cake, in a large bowl, cream together the oil, sugar, eggs, and vanilla with an electric mixer on high speed until light and well blended. Reduce to low speed and blend in the buttermilk.

Sift together the flour, cocoa, baking soda and powder, cinnamon, salt, and cloves in a medium-size bowl. Stir the flour mixture into the oil mixture just until the flour is moistened. Stir in the zucchini and spread the batter in the pan. Sprinkle the chocolate chips over the batter. Bake until a toothpick inserted into the center of the cake comes out clean, about 45 minutes. Cool completely and serve from the pan.

Cocoa Roll

MAKES ONE 12-INCH-LONG ROLL, OR 8 TO 10 SERVINGS

Every family has their favorite cake. In my husband's family it was pineapple upside-down cake. Ours was a chocolate cake with cocoa whipped cream. Barbara Leibert gave me her winning "Taste of Vermont" recipe many years ago when she and husband, Jerry, moved to Massachusetts to run the Windflower Inn in South Egremont, Massachusetts, with their daughter and son-in-law. Light and chocolaty, this versatile cake can be rolled or cut in thirds and layered. Filled and frozen, it can also be used like an ice cream cake. Now it has become the new favorite of our clan.

FOR THE CAKE

6 large eggs, separated

¼ teaspoon salt

¼ teaspoon cream of tartar

⅔ cup granulated sugar

8 ounces bittersweet chocolate, melted

2 tablespoons sifted unsweetened cocoa powder

FOR THE FILLING

1⅓ cups heavy cream

6 tablespoons confectioners' sugar, sifted

3 tablespoons unsweetened cocoa powder, sifted

1½ teaspoons pure vanilla extract

Preheat the oven to 350°F. Grease a jelly roll pan, line the pan with parchment paper, and grease and flour the paper, tapping out any excess flour.

To make the cake, in a large bowl, beat together the egg whites, salt, and cream of tartar with an electric mixer on high speed until soft peaks form. Gradually beat in the granulated sugar until a firm but not stiff meringue is formed. Stir the yolks into the melted chocolate. With a rubber spatula, mix one quarter of the meringue into the chocolate. Then fold the chocolate mixture into the remaining meringue.

Spread the mixture in the pan and bake until the surface of the cake feels dry, 15 to 20 minutes. Cool the cake in the pan. Sprinkle the cocoa on a piece of waxed paper as large as the cake. Loosen the edges of the cake with a knife and invert onto the paper.

To make the filling, whip the cream, confectioners' sugar, cocoa, and vanilla in a large bowl with an electric mixer on medium speed until stiff peaks form. Spread some of the filling over the cake and, using the waxed paper, tightly roll the cake up like a jelly roll starting with the long side. Frost with the remaining cocoa cream. Using two pancake spatulas, lift the cake onto a long serving platter. Serve the cake immediately or chill until serving time.

If using as an ice cream cake, wrap the filled cake well with plastic wrap and freeze up to 2 weeks. Remove from the freezer 20 minutes before serving.

COUNTRY TIPS AND TALES

When the Spanish conquered Mexico, they found the currency of the Aztecs was cacao beans. Montezuma, the Aztec emperor, received his tribute from each city in millions of the beans.

Applesauce Brownies

MAKES 16 BROWNIES

*F*rom the Farmers' Market, a book filled with wonderful recipes, sadly is out of print. Written by my dear friends Sandy Gluck and the late Richard Sax, it explores the expanding influence of regional farmers' markets in providing the direct connection of grower to buyer. This is an adaptation of one of their recipes. The applesauce keeps these cakey brownies moist.

3 squares (3 ounces) unsweetened chocolate

½ cup (1 stick) unsalted butter

1¼ cups all-purpose flour

1 teaspoon baking powder

½ teaspoon baking soda

¼ teaspoon salt

2 large eggs

1 cup firmly packed light brown sugar

1 teaspoon pure vanilla extract

1 cup unsweetened applesauce

1 cup coarsely chopped walnuts or pecans

Preheat the oven to 350°F. Grease a 9-inch-square baking pan. Melt the chocolate with the butter in a small heavy-bottomed saucepan over low heat. Sift together the flour, baking powder and soda, and salt in a small bowl. Whisk together the eggs, sugar, and vanilla in a large bowl. Stir the chocolate mixture into the egg mixture, then stir in the applesauce. Add the flour mixture and nuts and stir to combine. Spread the batter in the pan and bake until a toothpick inserted into the center of the cake comes out clean, about 25 minutes. Cool completely on a rack before cutting into squares.

COUNTRY TIPS AND TALES

O weary mothers mixing dough
Don't you wish food would grow?
Your lips would smile I know to see
A cookie bush or a pancake tree.
—Marthas Vineyard Hospital, *Island Cook Book*

Chocolate Potato Cake

MAKES 1 BUNDT CAKE, OR 16 TO 20 SERVINGS

High, moist, and a good keeper, this cake must have been devised by a clever cook who knew just what to do with leftover mashed potatoes. I have also made this with leftover sweet potatoes, to memorable effect. Bring this cake to the next bake sale.

2 large potatoes, peeled, cooked in water to cover until tender, drained
    and mashed (1½ cups)
4 squares (4 ounces) unsweetened chocolate, melted
1 cup (2 sticks) unsalted butter, at room temperature
2 cups firmly packed light brown sugar
1 teaspoon pure vanilla extract
4 large eggs
2 cups all-purpose flour
2 teaspoons baking powder
1 teaspoon baking soda
½ teaspoon salt
1 cup buttermilk
Confectioners' sugar

Preheat the oven to 350°F. Grease and flour a 10-inch Bundt pan. In a large bowl, mix the mashed potatoes and chocolate together with an electric mixer on low speed. Add the butter, sugar, and vanilla and beat on high speed until the mixture is light. Add the eggs, one at a time, scraping down the sides of the bowl after each addition. Stir together the flour, baking powder and soda, and salt together in a medium-size bowl and, on low speed, add alternately with the buttermilk.

Spread the batter evenly in the Bundt pan and bake until a toothpick inserted into the center of the cake comes out clean, about 1¼ hour. Cool completely in pan or on a rack. Carefully loosen the edges of the cake with a knife and invert onto a serving platter. Sprinkle with confectioners' sugar and serve.

Mail-Order Sources

Apple cider products

Willis and Tina Wood
Weatherfield Center Road
RD 2, Box 477
Springfield, Vermont 05156
(802) 263-5547

Cheese

Cabot Farmers Co-op Creamery
P.O. Box 128
Main Street
Cabot, Vermont 05647
(802) 563-3240

Grafton Village Cheese Co.
Townsend Road
P.O. Box 87
Grafton, Vermont 05146
(800) GRAFTON

The Seward Family
P.O. Box 218
East Wallingford, Vermont 05742
(802) 259-2311

Shelburne Farms
Farm Barn
Shelburne, Vermont 05482
(802) 985-8686

Flours and baking equipment

King Arthur Flour Baker's Catalogue
P.O. Box 876
Norwich, Vermont 05055
(800) 827-6836

Maple products

Fire Hill Farm
Andy Snyder and Chris Anderson
RR 2, Box 2392
Florence, Vermont 05744
(800) 69 SYRUP
Maple syrup, jams, jellies, pickles

Krueger-Norton Family
Trish Norton
Box 363
Cuttingsville, Vermont 05738
(802) 492-3638
Maple syrup, maple fudge

Maple Country Kitchen
Wilson and Sue Clark
RD 1, Box 310
Wells, Vermont 05774
(802) 325-3203
Maple syrup, maple butter, maple
cream, maple granules (sugar), jams,
and jellies

Spring Lake Ranch
Cuttingsville, Vermont 05738
(802) 492-3322
Maple syrup

Bibliography

A Lady. *The Housekeeper's Book*. Philadelphia: Williams, 1837 (facsimile ed., Somersworth, N.H.: New Hampshire Publishing, 1972).

Ball Corporation. *Ball Blue Book*. 32nd ed. Ball Corporation, Box 2005, Department WL, Muncie, Ind. 47307-0005.

Beard, James. *American Cookery*. Boston: Little, Brown, 1972.

Beeton, Mrs. Isabella. *The Book of Household Management*. London: S. O. Beeton, 1861 (facsimile ed., New York: Farrar, Straus & Giroux, 1969).

Bloch, Barbara. *The Meat Board Meat Book*. New York: McGraw-Hill, 1977.

Evans, T. M., and Greene, David. *The Meat Book*. New York: Scribner's, 1973.

Friends of the West Rutland Town Hall, Inc. *What's Been Cooking in West Rutland*. Lenexa Kans.: Cookbook Publishers, 1995.

Gewanter, V., and P. Parker. *Home Preserving Made Easy*. New York: Viking, 1975.

Giobbi, Edward. *Pleasures of the Good Earth*. New York: Knopf, 1991.

Goldstein, Roberta B. "Fling Jeweled Pebbles." *Rural Vermonter*, Vol. 2, Fall 1963.

Grigson, Jane. *Good Things*. New York: Atheneum, 1984.

Hale, William H., and *Horizon Magazine*, eds. *The Horizon Cookbook and Illustrated History of Eating and Drinking Through the Ages*. New York: American Heritage, 1968.

Hamlin, Suzanne. "Free Range? Natural? Sorting Out the Labels." *The New York Times*, November 13, 1996, sec. C1.

Harrison, Molly. *The Kitchen in History*. New York: Scribner's, 1972.

Hegi, Ursula. *Stones from the River*. New York: Scribner's, 1994.

Kander, Mrs. Simon. *The Settlement Cook Book*. Milwaukee: Settlement Cook Book Co., 1944.

Lafrance, M., and Y. Desloges. *Goûter à l'histoire*. Canada: Les éditions de la Chenelière, 1989.

Marthas Vineyard Hospital. *Island Cook Book*. Marthas Vineyard, Mass.: Herald Printing, 1924.

Masterton, E., and J. Masterton. *Nothing Whatever to Do*. New York: Crown, 1956.

Milne, A. A. *When We Were Very Young*. New York: Dutton, 1924.

Montagne, Prosper. *Larousse Gastronomique*. New York: Crown, 1961.

Nightingale, Marie. *Out of Old Nova Scotia Kitchens*. Canada: Nimbus, 1989.

Nimtz, S., and R. Cousineau. *Tomato Imperative!* New York: Little, Brown, 1994.

Ody, Penelope. *The Complete Medicinal Herbal*. London: Dorling Kindersley, 1993.

Oxford Dictionary of Quotations. 2nd ed. London: Oxford University Press, 1953.

Pearl, Mary. *Vermont Maple Recipes*. Burlington, Vt.: Lane Press, 1952.

Peden, Rachel. *Rural Free: A Farmwife's Almanac of Country Living*. New York: Knopf, 1961.

Phipps, Frances. *Colonial Kitchens, Their Furnishings, and Their Gardens*. New York: Hawthorn Books, 1972.

Pixley, Aristene. *Vermont Country Cooking*. New York: Dover, 1979.

Rosten, Leo. *Leo Rosten's Treasury of Jewish Quotations*. New York: McGraw-Hill, 1972.

Saint George's School. *Food for Thought*. Montreal: St. George's School, 1994.

Sax, Richard. *The Cookie Lover's Cookie Book*. New York: Harper & Row, 1986.

Sax, Richard, and Sandra Gluck. *From the Farmers' Market*. New York: Harper & Row, 1986.

Seely, H. *Fourth Report to the Vermont Board of Agriculture*. Montpelier, 1877.

Sheton, Ferne. *Pioneer Superstitions*. High Point, N.C.: Hutcraft, 1962.

Silitch, C., ed. *The Old Farmer's Almanac Colonial Cookbook*. Dublin, N.H.: Yankee, 1976.

United States Agriculture Department. *New England Agricultural Statistics*. Concord, N.H.: New England Agricultural Statistics Service, 1993.

University of Vermont Folklore Society. *Green Mountain Whittlin's*. Vols. 1–16. Burlington, Vt.: UVM Folklore Society, 1948–1966.

Vaughan, Beatrice. "From a Hill-Country Kitchen." *Rural Vermonter*, Fall 1963, pp. 34–35.

Vidler, Virginia. *Sugar-bush Antiques*. Cranbury, N.J.: A. S. Barnes and Co., 1979.

Volunteers of the Norwegian-American Museum. *Pioneer Cook Book*. Decorah, Iowa: Norwegian-American Museum, 1969.

Walton, E. P., ed., *Walton's Vermont Register*. Montpelier, published from 1830 through 1860.

Weiss, John. *Venison: From Field to Table*. New York: Outdoor Life, 1984.

Wigginton, Eliot, ed. *Foxfire 2*. New York: Anchor, 1973.

Women of St. Paul's Cathedral. *Out of Vermont Kitchens*, 11th ed., Burlington, Vt.: Women's Service League of St. Paul's Church, 1976.

Index

apple butter:
    pudding, steamed, 164–165
    spiced, 206–207
applesauce:
    brownies, 252–253
    walnut bars, 165–166
arrowroot, 1
Art of Cookery, The (King), 13
Austin, Jim, 71
Austin, Tom, 71, 72

B

bacon, 4
    and beans, town meeting, 40
bake, Maggie's cauliflower cheese, 78–79
baked:
    chocolate custard, 246
    fresh ham with garlic, 42
    ham with fall vegetables, 41
    maple apples, 162
    sour-cherry flan, 191–192
    squashes, little maple-, 147
Ball Blue Book, 157, 202
barbecue, parking lot chicken, 57
barley and mushroom–stuffed cabbage, 80–81
bars, applesauce walnut, 165–166
basil beans, hot, 156–157
basted pork roast, cider jelly-, 34–35
beans, dried, 3
    and bacon, town meeting, 40
    kale, and tomato casserole, 83
    soup, savory, 104–105
    see also green beans
Beaumont, Francis, 152
Beebe, Matt, 100
beef, 7–8
    boeuf à la mode, 17
    braised short ribs in cider, 20
    and Cheddar pie, 18–19
    corned, *see* corned beef
    flank steak sandwiches, 19
    herb-crusted roast, 10–11
    my favorite meat loaf, 38
    ragout of, 16

stew, old-fashioned, 15
    stock, 2
    Yankee pot roast, 12–13
beet(s):
    borscht, all-of-the-, 102–103
    Chris and Andy's maple-pickled, 150–151
    roasted, in honey-orange dressing, 149
Beeton, Isabella, 248
Biddle, Ludie, 25
Biddle, Stark, 25
biscuit(s):
    cornmeal, creamed turkey with, 62–63
    crust, for chicken pot pie, 45–46
    dried-apple, 122–123
    little leek, 124
    nutted squash drop, 121–122
    ragamuffins, 227
biscuit dough:
    for beef and Cheddar pie, 18–19
    caraway, for lamb pot pie with kohlrabi, 29
    for French-Canadian pork pie, 33–34
blackberry sugar tart, 194
Blaine, Maggie, 78
blueberry:
    buttermilk muffins, 126
    coffeecake, 198
    pancakes, Len's, 200
    poutine aux fraises et bluets, 188
    preserves, 202–203
    vanilla sauce, shortcake with, 196–197
boeuf à la mode, 17
boiled cider, 3, 146
    tartlets, 174–175
boiled dinner, Vermont, 14
Book of Household Management (Beeton), 248
borscht, all-of-the-beet, 102–103
bottom round roast, 10
braised:
    lamb shoulder, 26
    short ribs in cider, 20
    turkey, curry-, 64–65
bread(s):
    blueberry buttermilk muffins, 126
    brown-, muffins, 128
    buttermilk, 116–117
    Cheddar muffins, 127
    dried-apple biscuits, 122–123
    little leek biscuits, 124
    maple oatmeal, 114–115

crème fraîche, 3
crisp:
    apple oatmeal, 163
    strawberry-rhubarb, 190
crisp-fried rabbit, 70
crispy oven-fried chicken breasts, 56
crumb cake, raisin-pear, 181–182
cucumber pickles, Great-Grandma Hoff's sour
        crock, 154
Culpeper, Nicholas, 166
cupcakes, chocolate sauerkraut, 247–248
cup custards, maple, 224
currant:
    pie, fresh, 195–196
    and strawberry spoon pudding, 189
curry-braised turkey, 64–65
custard:
    baked chocolate, 246
    maple cup, 224
    sauce, hot chocolate pudding with, 244–245
Cutler, Sadie, 88, 101
cutlets, turkey, pan-fried, 63

D

dandelion-stuffed chicken breasts, 54–55
dark syrup vinegar cake with cardamom sauce,
        232–233
date pumpkin loaf, 212
dilled peas, and mushrooms, 148
doughnuts, Mom's, 129–130
dressing:
    honey-orange, roasted beets in, 149
    Mary's prize, kohlrabi salad with, 136–137
dried:
    -apple biscuits, 122–123
    beans, 3
    chestnuts, 3
    herbs, 4
    mushrooms, 4
    -pear drops, chewy, 177
drops, chewy dried-pear, 177
drunken lamb, Stark Biddle's, 25
dumplings:
    grandpère, 229–230

herbed, stewed chicken with, 48–49
strawberry, 193

E

Edwards, Jan, 24
eggplant moussaka, 31
eggs, 4

F

fallow deer, 72, 73
Fire Hill Farm, 150, 156
fish:
    chowder, ice-, 93
    smoked-, and potato dish, Friday night, 86
    stock, 2
flan:
    baked sour-cherry, 191–192
    de calabaza, 222–223
flank steak sandwiches, 19
flour, 4
Foxfire 2 (Wigginton), 67
French-Canadian pork pie, 33–34
fresh corn fritters, 135–136
fresh currant pie, 195–196
fresh ham with garlic, baked, 42
fricassee, chicken, 52–53
Friday night smoked-fish and potato dish, 86
fritters, fresh corn, 135–136
From the Farmers' Market (Gluck and Sax), 252
frosting, maple cream, cinnamon cake with,
        230–231
fruit desserts:
    apple and Cheddar pie, 171–172
    apple oatmeal crisp, 163
    applesauce walnut bars, 165–166
    apple upside-down cake, 168
    baked maple apples, 162
    baked sour-cherry flan, 191–192
    blackberry sugar tart, 194

pie with cream, 182–183
-raisin crumb cake, 181–182
and rice pudding, stirred, 178–179
Peden, Rachel, 132
peppers, carrots, and cauliflower, sweet-and-sour, 155
pepper steak, venison, 71
Perry, Thelma, 41
pickled beets, Chris and Andy's maple-, 150–151
pickles:
bread and butter summer squash, 152–153
Great-Grandma Hoff's sour crock, 154
pie:
apple and Cheddar, 171–172
caramel apple, 172–173
fresh currant, 195–196
lattice-topped squash and apple, 219–220
maple buttermilk, 234–235
pear, with cream, 182–183
pear-mincemeat, 184–185
pumpkin ginger, 217–218
pie, savory:
beef and Cheddar, 18–19
chicken pot, 45–46
French-Canadian pork, 33–34
lamb pot, with kohlrabi, 28–29
North Country onion, 84–85
shepherd's, with turnip-potato crust, 30–31
succotash, 76–77
Pioneer Cook Book, 189
Pioneer Superstitions (Sheton), 49, 115
polenta, 4–5
Polish cabbage and sausage, 39
pork, 8–9
baked fresh ham with garlic, 42
baked ham with fall vegetables, 41
chops, apple-and-onion-stuffed, 36
pie, French-Canadian, 33–34
roast, cider jelly–basted, 34–35
and squash stew, harvest, 37
see also sausage
potato(es):
chocolate cake, 254
garden colcannon, 143
hodgepodge, 81–82
salad, Shrewsbury, 141
scalloped, 142
and smoked-fish dish, Friday night, 86

soup, Grandma's, 101–102
-turnip crust, shepherd's pie with, 30–31
pot pie:
chicken, 45–46
for a crowd, baking, 46
lamb, with kohlrabi, 28–29
pot roast, Yankee, 12–13
potted rabbit, 69
poutine aux fraises et bluets, 188
preserves:
blueberry, 202–203
quince, 201–202
strawberry-rhubarb, 204
pudding:
butternut squash, 221
hot chocolate, with custard sauce, 244–245
poutine aux fraises et bluets, 188
steamed apple-butter, 164–165
stirred pear and rice, 178–179
strawberry and currant spoon, 189
pudding, savory:
green chile, corn, and rice, 87
sweet corn and chive, 134
pumpkin:
almond cake, 214
date loaf, 212
flan de calabaza, 222–223
ginger pie, 217–218
and molasses cake, spicy, 215–216
nutted squash drop biscuits, 121–122
-orange rolls, 120–121
puree, 213

Q

Quigley, Jane, 184
quince preserves, 201–202

R

rabbit, 44
cacciatore, 67–68

Trish's maple cream fudge, 225
turkey:
    breast, apple and walnut–stuffed, 60–61
    Cheddar burgers, 64
    creamed, with cornmeal biscuits, 62–63
    curry-braised, 64–65
    cutlets, pan-fried, 63
    roast, with sausage stuffing, 58–60
turnip:
    -potato crust, shepherd's pie with,
        30–31
    see also rutabaga

U

upside-down cake:
    apple, 168–169
    raspberry topsy-turvy, 199

V

vanilla, 5
    blueberry sauce, shortcake with, 196–197
Vaughan, Beatrice, 131
vegetable(s):
    fall, baked ham with, 41
    hodgepodge, 81–82
    stock, 2
venison:
    chili, spicy, 74
    chops, 72–73
    pepper steak, 71
Vermont:
    boiled dinner, 14
    cheese, 3
vinegar cake with cardamom sauce, dark syrup,
    232–233

W

Wallingford Locker hams, 41
walnut(s):
    applesauce bars, 165–166
    and apple–stuffed turkey breast, 60–61
    gratin of zucchini and, 79
    maple-nut sticky buns, 228–229
    maple sundaes, 226
    -onion-rye rolls, 118–119
Wells, Michael, 24
Welsh lamb with cloves, 24
Wetherby, Hazel, 177
whole-wheat:
    Italian loaves, my half-, 113–114
    raisin bread, Rob's, 111–112
Wigginton, Eliot, 67
wild leeks (ramps), rabbit sautéed with, 66
Windflower Inn, 25
Woodchuck cider, 20, 21
Woods, Tina, 34, 146
Woods, Willis, 34, 146

Y

Yankee pot roast, 12–13
yeast, 5
Yukon Gold potatoes, 30

Z

zucchini:
    bread and butter summer squash pickles,
        152–153
    chocolate-chip cake, 249
    and walnuts, gratin of, 79